Solomon's Song

A 90 Day Journey of
God's Expressed Desire
For Your Heart

By: Daniel Stombaugh

May you live forever FROM HIS love.
Daniel Stombaugh
Eph 3:14-20

CANNONPUBLISHING

Solomon's Song

*A 90 Day Journey of
God's Expressed Desire
For Your Heart*

By: Daniel Stombaugh

CANNONPUBLISHING

Published by: Cannon Publishing.
Cannon Publishing P.O. Box 1298
Greenville, NC 27835
Author owns complete rights to this book and may be contacted
in regards to distribution.

Printed in the United States of America

First Printing, 2015

ISBN-13:978-1515162254

ISBN-10:1515162257

Ordering Information:

Quantity Sales. Special discounts are available on quantity
purchases by corporations, associations, and others via
www.DanielStombaugh.com

Book Cover Design: Bobby Barnhill
Editorial Services: Cannon Publishing
Formatting Services: Marsena Cook

Book Dedication

This book is dedicated to my wife Angela, and my three ridiculously awesome children Clark, Brynn, and Blake, who make every minute of my life worthwhile.

You each in your own unique relationship with me have taught me how to understand the Father's relentless desire for my heart.

Introduction

Is it possible that a single letter could change a person's life?

I remember reading a story a while back about a family in England who had taken a family heirloom chair to be reupholstered. As the craftsman began to work on the chair he made a startling discovery. Inside the arm of the chair was an old letter which had been folded to the size of a small coin. The letter was written in an older style French language and it was dated to be roughly 200 years old. When it was deciphered, the letter turned out to be a love letter between two unknown people whose identities remain a mystery to this day.

Here's what the letter said:

"My dear small love, do not be worried, do you seriously believe I would tell anything to these people who don't understand anything about love?"

"If someone insists that I say something, it will be anything but the dear love acquired by you, which is the great treasure hidden in my heart."

"At the moment I write this letter, I can hear my aunt yelling; who else annoys us all day long, today and tomorrow."

"My dear, I cover you with kisses and caresses until… I need you in this moment of desire. I love you."

While we do not know the identities of the parties involved, nor the circumstances in the need to hide the letter, what we do know is that there was passion involved and it was expressed in a way that was extremely personal to the person to whom it was written.

I love the story of this letter because this book you are holding is really about another love letter that is much older than 200 years.

Unlike the first letter mentioned here, neither the details of this letter nor the intended audience remain a mystery. I want to re-introduce you to this letter and how I believe it will change your life over the next ninety days. I say this with confidence, because this letter has changed everything about mine.

There was a season in my life when I experienced a difficult time in my heart and was in a place where I was second guessing my value to God and to those in my life. I craved closeness and intimacy and began to pour my heart out to God and asked Him to change others in my life in order to meet my needs for love and affirmation. It was in this time of questioning that I felt God's Spirit say, *"Dan, You are asking what everyone does. You are asking me to meet your needs through a source other than me. Ask me to meet your needs in me alone."*

So I did, and what you are about to embark on is a ninety day journey of what He showed me because of the simple request, *"God, please tell me how do you feel about me?"*

The Apostle Paul writes a fascinating statement which is found in the third chapter of Ephesians that if he could get one message out to the bride (the church) it would be this, *"You are loved!"*

I believe one of the biggest and most effective weapons that Satan uses is the weapon of rejection. People truly are seeking love and like the prodigal son they will travel to every town and every empty well in search of identity and the love that will only come from knowing who you are in Christ and who you are to the Father.

I asked God to allow me to find true significance, true security and true love in Him and He directed me to read the Song of Solomon. Although I had grown up in the church, I had never heard much taught on the Song of Solomon, so the fact I now held this portion of the Bible open in my hands was strange.

As I read this portion of scripture, I felt God speak to my heart in every passage in a way that was deeply personal and in the fashion of a love letter from God to me. I wrote them down as I read through the Song of Solomon and by the time I was through reading, I held the ninety letters that you now hold. I believe the Song of Solomon is about more than a king and a shepherd girl. I believe this is a love letter where The King of Kings expresses His heart's desire for us as His bride.

By way of introduction, I want to list out the very first passage from the Song of Solomon to explain how to get the most from this devotional.

"The song of songs, which is Solomon's." ~**Song of Solomon 1:1**

The very first verse of this song says it all. Most people miss it because they fail to ask the right questions when they read.

Solomon was making a claim about this song called "The Song of Solomon" and it seems to be a pretty fantastic claim.

This is the Song of Songs. In other words, what you are about to read is the best song that has ever been written and will ever be written.

I then had to ask the question, *"What makes a great song great?"* Is it the melody, or the lyrics? Pause and think about that for a moment.

I submit to you it is neither the melody nor the lyrics that makes a great song great, but rather it is the message of a song which makes it great.

Solomon is claiming the message in this song is what makes it the greatest song that has ever been or ever will be sung.

BETWEEN THE MELODY AND THE LYRICS YOU WILL FIND THE MESSAGE.

The message of a song lies between the melody and the lyrics and in order to hear the message you almost have to train yourself to look beyond what your eyes initially see.

You cannot allow yourself to stay on the surface of what you read in the lyrics or listen to in the melody. You must ask yourself as you hear this song unfold, *"What are you trying to tell me? "What is the message that you have for me in this song?"*

As we look at this song, you are going to see words and you are going to hear a melody, but you will also be blown away as you are reminded of God's love and just how much and deeply He loves you. Do not allow yourself be robbed of the message regarding God's heart for you by focusing on the shepherd girl, or the king in this story.

Solomon claims that this writing is better than anything that David has ever written, or that he himself has ever written. I Kings Chapter 4 tells us that Solomon wrote 1,005 songs and we know King David, his father, wrote even more and yet this song you are about to experience over the next ninety days is the greatest song and message you will ever hear.

This book you are holding is an answer to my prayer asking the King of Kings to explain His heart for me. The entire book of the Song of Solomon has been broken down passage by passage into ninety individual and daily "love letters" from the King to us, and I cannot wait for you to witness God's love letters as you read and know there is also a place for you to daily correspond and write your own letter back to God in light of what He reveals to you in regards to His heart for you. God bless you as you read His expressed desire for your heart.

~Dan

Day 1

> *"Kiss me again and again, for your love is sweeter than wine."*
> ~ **Song of Solomon 1:2**
>
> In this passage the shepherd girl is expressing to the king the realization of his love for her surpasses the satisfaction any temporal source could provide. The picture is beautiful to us because as we grow in our understanding of The King's love for us, the desire for satisfaction in outside sources diminishes.

My Love,

A kiss is amazingly powerful. Wars have been started and ended with a single kiss and the passion it represents. The thing that makes this physical expression so powerful is when it is given and received willingly. It is a precursor to something that follows which is much more connected and meaningful. It speaks of a bond that is forged within, unable to be broken in spite of the harshest of blows that life can bring.

Wine is valued because of its ability when consumed to relax and cause the one who drinks to forget. It alters the true and existing reality and can create a false sense of security, warmth, bravery, and love.

I love you.

My love for you is very strong and intense. I want to willingly express how much I love you and when you willingly receive the love that I desire to express to you the bond between us will truly withstand the fires of hell and the fury with which it assaults you.

My love for you will transform your heart, soul and mind into a place where no outside source could hope to. The temporal effects of wine will wear off and fade. The faces you seek to find a substitute for my love in will age and turn away for they were never meant to fill the place within you that I saw from the first day I looked into your eyes.

No other source can satisfy the thirst within you. Can't you see how every path you have taken in your life has led you to me? Every time the effects of the wines you have chosen to satisfy you have worn off, I have been here waiting patiently to satisfy and complete you.

I love you, and you are valuable to me! Let my love for you become your source and your strength. You were made to be loved by me.

Love,
The King

Date _____

_____

_____

_____

_____

_____

_____

_____

_____

_____

_____

_____

_____

_____

_____

_____

_____

_____

_____

Day 2

> *"Because of the savor of thy good ointments thy name is as ointment poured forth, therefore do the virgins love thee."*
>
> ## ~ Song of Solomon 1:3
>
> The shepherd girl is comparing the name of the king with a beautiful fragrance. As a believer you can identify the ways that the name of The King fills your heart with joy. Meditating on His acts of goodness in your life has a fragrance that causes you to follow Him wherever He leads.

My Love,

I want you to take just a moment to breathe me in. Have you ever noticed how different fragrances bring different feelings to the surface of your mind's awareness?

A rose, a newborn baby, a candle, clean clothes, a rainstorm, the ocean, pumpkin pie, coffee, a turkey dinner, and even bacon?

What comes to your mind is a memory of an interaction you had with the source of that smell. Good or bad, you will always be brought into a direct confrontation every single time that sense is engaged.

I want you to take just a moment to breathe me in and tell me what comes to mind.

What feelings and emotions are brought to the surface of your mind's awareness as you say my name and smell my scent in your life?

What do I evoke in you? Do you inhale the scent of me as your protector? I want you to take a moment and think back to all of the times where I literally protected you from harm.

Do you inhale the scent of me as your comforter? Do you remember when you were at your lowest point and I walked in and embraced you? What kind of things do you think about as you breathe me in? What attributes of mine do you immediately think of when you take in my fragrance?

Power? Strength? Vigilance? Creator? Healer?

I am everything you need and I want to be your first choice in any situation and circumstance that you face.

The more you understand what my name means, because of the different things that you go through with me, the more you will see just how much I truly love you.

You will understand how everything I've allowed into your life was done so that you were able to see all of me in the midst of it. I have been drawing you to me through my name.

The reason people are willing to experience adversity, overcome them or even lose everything they own in the process is because they have discovered me through the names they have seen. Smell me today.

Breathe me in! I am close enough for you to inhale and when you do, please know that I belong to you and you belong to me. For I am madly in love with you.

Love,
The King

Day 3

When the understanding sinks in to the shepherd girl she was chosen to be in the chambers with the king, there is nothing that could draw her away from him. The King of Kings chose you to experience a relationship with Him. He called you to Him and you responded. You now stand in His presence completely loved and nothing can ever change your present position with Him.

My Love,

I love you and I love where you are standing in this very moment. In front of me!

I cannot help but feel intensity in my very core as I take the sight of you in because I brought you here past so many barricades and walls.

Many people share my attention, but you share my personal chamber. This level of engagement and intimacy is one that can only be made possible via my approval; and you, my love, have my approval.

It is my privilege to have you in this room with me, and I am a richer king because you are here.

In my chamber you are going to learn who I am and I will show you who you are to me. I will give you my strength, and my confidence. You will never be the same.

As we grow in this relationship together, you will forever continue to fall in love with me.

You are mine,
The King

Day 4

> *"I am black, but comely, o ye daughters of Jerusalem, as the tents of Kedar, as the curtains of Solomon."*
>
> ## ~ Song of Solomon 1:5~
>
> As she stands before the king, the shepherd girl does what each of us do when The King holds us in His gaze. She presents every reason why the king should not love her and why she fails to deserve the kingdom privileges that he allows her to enjoy. The fabric she compares herself to is heavy, dark, and skin irritating material. The king quickly reminds her that he made her silk just as The King reminds us that He made us new.

My Love,

I want you to know at this very moment you are exactly what I desire.

I know there are times in which you look at those around you and see things about them that you feel would make you more appealing or somehow more worthy of the love that I give to you, but this is not the truth.

The very things about you that make you cringe inside are the very things that make you so attractive to me. In a sea of people I will always search for you because my kingdom would not be what it was made to be without you in it.

I want to spend eternity telling you how taken I am with you.

When you found me, I made you strong. I made you beautiful and secure. You are funny, amazingly brilliant, and the things that you come up with off the top of your head make me laugh. You are smart. You are confident, strong, and brave.

I love the way you get so passionately worked up about things that are important to you and the way your eyes fill with light when you talk about the things you love. You are loyal, real, and most importantly of all, you are mine!

You enchant me and I have waited forever for you to notice me. You are silk to me; elegant, soft, and you were tailor made for this king!

All my heart,
The King

Date _____

_____
_____
_____
_____
_____
_____
_____
_____
_____
_____
_____
_____
_____
_____
_____
_____
_____
_____

Day 5

My Love,

When you look into my eyes I can see your very soul.

You have experienced much hurt in your life; and as you stand before me, I see your insecurities rise up within you, and you wish that you could have presented me a returned love that was somehow more worthy.

Today I would like for you to do something that may be very difficult for you to do. I want you to go about your day knowing that you are exactly what I have always wanted. Know that the things about you in which you feel should be different are the very things which cause me to notice you.

Your imperfections are what make you perfect for me; and it is the very things that you feel make you weak, that prove to both of us how much we were meant to be together. I want to give you my strength where you are the weakest. Please know that anytime you are tempted to compare yourself with another, I will be right here waiting to remind you that you are perfect.

Today I want you to operate out of my opinion of you and not your own.

You are mine; and I am willing to move Heaven and Earth to prove to you that you are exactly who and what I have always wanted and desired.

All my heart,
The King

Date _____

_____

_____

_____

_____

_____

_____

_____

_____

_____

_____

_____

_____

_____

_____

_____

_____

_____

_____

_____

_____

Day 6

> *"Tell me, o thou whom my soul loveth, where thou feedest, where thou makest thy flock to rest at noon: for why should I be as one that turneth aside by the flocks of thy companions? If thou knowest not, o fairest among women, go thy way forth by the footsteps of the flock, and feed thy kids beside the shepherds tents."*
>
> ## ~ Song of Solomon 1:7-8~
>
> The shepherd girl desires to be wherever the king is and she is not content to hear about his activities from others. Her desire is to experience his activities first hand. The more you understand The King the less you will be content to hear of others experiences with Him. You will desire to learn of Him by daily interaction.

My Love,

One of my favorite times of the day with you is in the early morning. Your eyes softly flutter open, and I watch as you become aware of your surroundings. In that very moment I see what your heart tries so hard to express to me during your day.
I see you. I see the real you. I see the side of you that you may feel that no one sees and you wish you could articulate to me. I know you love me and you may feel inadequate in the expression of your love to me. I know you want to be around me and that you crave time with me; and that, my love, is truly amazing.

You are not content to hear about me from other people who know me. I know in the deepest recesses of your soul, no matter what you may say or do occasionally, you truly do desire me. You are mine from the tip of your toe to the top of your head and I am blown away by your heart for me. This is why I wait expectantly each morning, just as I did today, to see your eyes open. I see your love for me in your eyes right in the moment they begin to bring your surroundings into focus.

Before you put your feet on the floor this morning and start your day with all of the twists and turns it will bring. Before all of the noise and distractions; please, just take a deep breath and let me look into your eyes again. I love you and you are truly amazing to me! Focus just a moment on what I see in you. Know within your heart I truly see you, and what I see blows me away.

All my love,
The King

Date _____

_____
_____
_____
_____
_____
_____
_____
_____
_____
_____
_____
_____
_____
_____
_____
_____
_____
_____
_____

Day 7

> *"I have compared thee, o my love, to a company of horses in Pharaoh's Chariots."*
>
> ## ~ Song of Solomon 1:9~~
>
> Horses were looked at with value in Solomon's court because of the sheer expense in bringing them from across the globe into his kingdom. The King of Kings spared no expense to bring you into His presence and you are looked at with extreme value to Him.

My Love,

Today I want you to know you are valuable to me. You look around at everything I possess yet miss just what it is that truly makes me a rich king. It is the fact you stand before me in my presence. It is our relationship that makes me wealthy. Ever since I saw you for the first time, I had to have you for myself.

You were unaware I was watching you, and as you were speaking to someone across the room; and when my name came up, I saw you smile.

That did it. I was captivated and nothing in Heaven or on Earth was going to prevent me from pursuing this relationship.

No obstacle was too big and no stain was too deep. Don't you know that I would go to the ends of the earth to bring you to me?

Don't you know how my heart aches to have you look at me, and don't you realize how quickly my heart melts when you speak my name?

I long to be your source and to protect and defend you, and I have prepared the very best of places for you to live and the very finest of things to fulfill your every need.

All I own seems empty without you to enjoy it with me. I do not expect you to understand this love I have for you; I only ask for you to accept it.

Today, walk in your value to me; knowing no matter who or what would try to tell you any differently, you have made me a wealthier king.

Eternally yours,
The King

Date _____

_____

_____

_____

_____

_____

_____

_____

_____

_____

_____

_____

_____

_____

_____

_____

_____

_____

Day 8

"Thy cheeks are comely with rows of jewels, thy neck with chains of gold. We will make thee borders of gold with studs of silver."

~ Song of Solomon 1:10-11~

In this passage, King Solomon assures his bride that he will cover any flaws that she may have within herself, with his power and wealth. God frames in our faults with His grace, and when we look at the areas in our life where we feel lack, we cannot help but see His power and mercy surrounding us. He completes us just as the king longed to complete the shepherd girl.

My Love,

You work so hard to try to hide things about yourself you feel have caused you to become flawed.
Don't you see how I long to add to you?

I want to add me to you; and in that addition, you will find true completion.

I accentuate everything that you are. It is my power and grace that frames your hurts and causes those very flaws to become your greatest picture of beauty.

I will make you to be everything that you wish you could be, and I will help you to far surpass anything that you could ever hope to become.

Do not resist me. Let me take you and help you to see in yourself what I have always seen. I am madly in love with who you were, are, and who you will one day become. Trust me with those areas of insecurity you try to hide.

Trust me with your fears, dreams, hopes and the feelings you guard so much.

I love you with all of my heart, my beautiful one; and I will not stop working to show you just how incredibly breathtaking you are to me!

Eternally,
The King

Date _____

Day 9

> *"While the king sitteth at his table, my spikenard sendeth forth the smell thereof. A bundle of myrrh is my beloved unto me; he shall lie all night betwixt my breasts."*
>
> **~ Song of Solomon 1:12-13~**
>
> The king desired to be with the shepherd girl because he enjoyed her company. Her words were fragrant to him and he was captivated with everything about her. God desires your company and He finds complete satisfaction in you. He provided a means for you to experience a relationship with Him because He genuinely enjoys your presence. Your prayers are fragrant to Him. You are enough.

My Love,

One of my favorite times is just being able to be next to you. I watch you as you go about your day and I listen to the words of your life's song and I am mesmerized.

I inhale you, and the fragrance you give off is captivating. I am satisfied with you, and there is nothing that stirs my heart like having you in my presence.

I chose you because you satisfy me. I anticipate every encounter we have because I desire to convey to you in each moment just how much I value what you bring to the relationship in your simple acceptance of the love I desire to lavish on you.

I love to touch your life because every time I do, it reminds me of every other moment we shared when I touched your life.

Memories flood my mind of times we have had together and inspire me for times we will continue to have in our relationship. I truly have loved you before time began and will continue to love you long after time ends.

Today I want you to be aware that just as you thrill to recognize when I interact with you, I thrill as well. This is how we communicate and this is the special bond of relationship we share. Together is so much better because of you.

My Heart,
The King

Date _____

_____

_____

_____

_____

_____

_____

_____

_____

_____

_____

_____

_____

_____

_____

_____

_____

_____

_____

_____

_____

_____

_____

Day 10

> *"My beloved is unto me as a cluster of camphire in the vineyards of Engedi."*
>
> **~ Song of Solomon 1:14~**
>
> Solomon makes a comparison to a particular flower called a Rock Rose, and the garden he refers to was at one time a barren wasteland. Solomon, in his power, created a beautiful and lush garden where hundreds of plants were transported to out of their natural environment and nurtured into growth. The Rock Rose grows from a rock and likewise you and I grow from The Solid Rock. We were taken from our natural environment and planted in Christ and in that growth we are a testimony to the power of The King and His tender nurturing care.

My Love,

You are so unique to me. You are my flower and you are a beautiful and delicate reminder to the world that true beauty really does exist.

You stand out from everything and everyone around you. What was once a dry and lonely place now radiates the very essence of life to me because you allowed me to bring you here with me. You let me transplant you from your natural surroundings to this place where I can now enjoy seeing you every day.

I made you to be seen and admired because everything about you reflects and expresses me.

When your talents blossom to their fullest, you emanate a fragrance to everyone around you that forces them to stop and take notice of you. It is in that moment that you are able to display who it is that planted you where you are planted. Every color that you display in your personality and actions is enhanced and deepened by my love for you.

The love that I have for you enriches and deepens the fragrance and the shades of your bloom.

Stand up today and display your smile. Display me in the garden where I have planted you. Allow people to see how only I can create such beauty in a place where there was none to be found.

I have an eye for genuine beauty and you, my love, have my eye.

Love,
The King

Date _____

_____
_____
_____
_____
_____
_____
_____
_____
_____
_____
_____
_____
_____
_____
_____
_____
_____
_____
_____

Day 11

My Love,

I love it when you look at me, when you speak with me. There is such a gentle rhythm that comes from deep within you, and it makes me glad this music can exist between souls.

You are perfect just the way you are but I know you feel there are so many things about you that need to be changed. Listen very carefully when I say you attract me just as you are.

The more you rest in me, the more you will learn who you are and who I made you to be when I brought you into the palace. Rest in the fact I see your heart and I love what I see.

Take time today to look up into my eyes and let me enjoy what it is that I see when I look into yours.

Let me see your questions, burdens, mistakes and fears.

Trust me with your gaze and know that I am looking with the express purpose to heal, restore, repair, and renew.

I love looking into your eyes because your eyes reveal the real you, and the real you is who I choose to passionately pursue!

My heart's desire,
The King

Day 12

> *"Behold, thou art fair, my beloved, yea, pleasant: also our bed is green. The beams of our house are cedar, and our rafters of fir."*
>
> ### ~ Song of Solomon 1:16-17~
>
> The beauty of this passage is found in its implication. Solomon desires relationship with his bride outside the confines of the places you would expect to experience it. The spiritual implication is an invitation from The King to seek interaction with Him outside of the confines of the expected times and places. Seek Him in our day to day activities and experience our lives with Him.

My Love,

I wanted a relationship with you.

I do not want our relationship to be confined within the walls of the pre-planned and the expected. I do not want what we share to be contained within the walls of a building for a few hours of a week. I want to walk with you throughout your day.

I want to sing along with you as you vacuum the carpets and laugh with you and at the faces you make in the mirrors as you walk by them.

When you create a culinary masterpiece in the kitchen, I want to be there with you to experience that as well.

When you are alone and hurting, I want to be there to hold you and comfort you until you are patched up and good to go at life again. When you are sick, let me be there to heal you and care for you.

When you are afraid, let me protect you. When you feel as though no one will listen, let me hear you. When you are sad, let me uplift you; and when you are discouraged, let me inspire you.

I want a relationship in which you can be secure with no limits or confines. You can take me everywhere and anywhere with you and ask me anything.

You are mine and our relationship will never be limited to one place or time because my love and desire for you are eternal.

Yours,
The King

Date _____

_____

_____

_____

_____

_____

_____

_____

_____

_____

_____

_____

_____

_____

_____

_____

_____

_____

_____

_____

Day 13

> *"I am the rose of Sharon, and the Lilly of the valleys."*

> **~ Song of Solomon 2:1~**

> The shepherd girl has declared her acceptance of her new identity, and this is what The King of Kings desires for us; to live and operate from the understanding that we have His affirmation and no longer from the attempt to earn His affirmation. We are not what we feel. We are who His word reveals us to be. Our identity is in Him now, and we are royalty.

My Love,

The greatest day of your life will be discovered in the very moment you choose to operate in the way I see you. You are no longer what you once were, and everything you have done up to this very moment has served as a vehicle to bring you closer to me. You are mine and you are exactly what I have always wanted.

I do not want you to live in the past, and I no longer want you to rehearse the pain and disappointments you have previously experienced.

Take a moment and look around the chamber that you now share with me and be fully be aware of the fact that this is your "Now." The "now" is where I want you to live with me.

The past is gone. It may or may not have happened the way you planned it but live in the moment of discovery knowing that you are exactly what I have always wanted and desired you to be. I want you just as you are.

You are so beautiful and you bloom in a way that stirs my heart. You, at this very moment, demonstrate to everyone around you my love and attention have made you confident and strong. You bloom and flourish from our relationship.

You are mine, my love, and my heart waits for the day you fully accept and live *"from"* my affirmation and not *"for"* my affirmation. I see you as complete!

Live in this moment with me. What have I made you? Who could ever hope to change this?

Today I want you to make a clean break with your past and trust me with your now.

                              All of my heart,
                              The King

Date _____

_____

Day 14

> *"As the Lilly among the thorns, so is my love among the daughters."*
>
> ### ~ Song of Solomon 2:2~
>
> Solomon was telling his bride she stood out to him and she had his eye. You have The King's eye. He is very much aware of you and you will face nothing of which He will not be aware.
> You hold His gaze and His attention.

My Love,

You stand out. You always have and you always will. There is just no comparison because everything about you makes you completely unique.

Have I mentioned just how much I love uniqueness?

What makes you stand out to me and what catches my attention is the way you speak, and what really holds me is the way your heart pronounces your words.

You were made to speak to my heart. I hear the words that you feel that no one thinks you have the ability to express. Your heart makes you stand out to me.

When I look across a crowded room, my gaze is fixed upon you and I smile every time you become aware that I am watching you.

I truly want everyone you come in contact with to be able to see the person that I see. Even those closest to you miss out on you, but please understand that I do see you.

I can't get enough of you!

Love,
The King

Date _____

Day 15

> *"As the apple tree among the trees of the wood, so is my beloved among the sons. I sat down under his shadow with great delight, and his fruit was sweet to my taste."*

~ Song of Solomon 2:3~

The bride is describing her groom, the king. He delights her with the entirety of who he is. Likewise The King provides shelter, nourishment, protection, and care for us; and He longs to demonstrate His ability to do so.

My Love,

I want to stand out to you. I want you to notice everything I am for you.

I am strength for your weakness. I am balance for your highs and I am encouragement for your lows.

I am shade when you are tired and a covering from the rain. I live to satisfy any desire you may have and today I call to you to draw close to me.

I will protect you. You have nothing to fear. You are safe and secure with me. I will never hurt you. My desire is for you to know me deeply. Open your heart to me. Let me have all of you and accept all of me. What you will find in all of me is all you will ever need. I am your protection. I am your provision. I am your source.

Love,
The King

Day 16

> *"He brought me into his banqueting house, and his banner over me was love."*
>
> **~ Song of Solomon 2:4~**
>
> Solomon brought his bride into his house. She now had access to everything that the king had at his disposal and the banqueting house was a place of celebration and provision. His name was on the banner over the place where he sat; and when she saw his name imprinted over her she understood that she was his and under his protection. God brought you into His kingdom and His name is love. He covers you under the authority and power of His name and you are safe.

My Love,

When I began this relationship with you, two very important things took place and I never want these to ever leave your heart or mind. The first is the fact I am yours completely and wholly. I cover you with my name as well as my love. The second fact is that you are mine. You belong to me from the top of your head to the sole of your foot. I jealously protect what is mine with a consuming passion.

Today I want you to take a moment to understand you are covered by my love. It is your strength and protection. Nothing can penetrate this bond or breach this wall. It is everything I am, have been, or ever will be.

I will always provide for you and when I took you for myself, I in turn met every single need you will ever have. In every circumstance you have ever found yourself in, while you were looking for help, I was there all the time and I was covering you.

Feel my protective love in all you do throughout your day and know this love I have for you is inexhaustible.

The greatest possessions in this life cannot be seen or heard as much as felt within your heart.

Today I long for you to feel my love for you.

Yours eternally
The King

Date _____

_____

_____

_____

_____

_____

_____

_____

_____

_____

_____

_____

_____

_____

_____

_____

_____

_____

_____

_____

_____

Day 17

> *"Stay with me flagon, comfort me with apples:*
> *for I am sick of love."*
> **~Song of Solomon 2:5~**
>
> The bride is overwhelmed by how she feels in response to the way the king expresses his love to her. Ten thousand little things have caught her attention about the king since she first entered the palace and his displays of affection leave her in a place where she is lovesick. What has God done for you today as part of His ten thousand displays of affection for you? Think about the depth of love that God provides you with and allow yourself the freedom to be overwhelmed.

My Love,

I want to remind you of something that is easily forgotten with everything that happens throughout the course of your day.

My love for you is patient.

My love for you is kind.

My love for you does not envy and it does not boast. It is not proud, nor is it rude.

My love for you is not self-seeking.

My love for you is not easily angered and it keeps no records of wrongdoing.

My love does not delight in evil, but it does rejoice with the truth.

My love for you will always protect, trust, hope,
and persevere.

My love for you allows me to bear all things for you.

My love for you believes all things, hopes all things, and will endure all things.

The love that I have for you will never end, and it will never fail.

I need you to know this today. It is the knowledge of this that will comfort you and sustain you when you feel weak and overwhelmed. It will restore you when you are exhausted in your heart.

I am here, and I will never leave you. Ever.

Everything that I am,
The King

Date _____

_____
_____
_____
_____
_____
_____
_____
_____
_____
_____
_____
_____
_____
_____
_____
_____
_____
_____

Day 18

> *"His left hand is under my head, and his right hand doth embrace me."*
>
> **~ Song of Solomon 2:6~**
>
> The picture here is beautiful. The king is resting with his bride and his left hand holds her head close to his chest where his heartbeat can be heart. When you allow yourself to tune out the noise around you and listen to the heartbeat of God for you, you become very aware of His protective nature in His right hand. He holds you close to Himself and you are safe in His unfailing arms. The heartbeat of The King will always remind you of the protection of The King.

My Love,

Today I want nothing more than to just hold you close to me. I want you to listen for my heartbeat. Listen to the rhythm as it beats for you and understand that I want you to know me.

I crave relationship with you because you satisfy me. The more that you grow in your understanding of my love for you, the more that you will find that I am able to satisfy any need you will ever have because I am security, strength, significance, and intimacy.

My love for you is not self-seeking.

Rest in me today and listen for my heartbeat in every sound you hear today. It is beyond audible!

Listen for me in the songs you hear, in the people you speak with, and even in the words you will find yourself giving to other people. As you listen you will discover, in the time we have shared, I have completely saturated you with myself and my heart's deepest expression of love.

Listen today and allow yourself to be satisfied by me.

All for you,
The King

Day 19

> *"I charge you, O ye daughters of Jerusalem, by the roes, and by the hinds of the field, that ye stir not up, nor awake my love, till he please."*
>
> **~ Song of Solomon 2:7~**
>
> The king is resting with his bride here and the picture given here is an amazing portrayal of what our relationship with The King should look like. The invitation of The King is an invitation to rest with Him in the completed work of your salvation. This is the true test of a relationship; can you trust Him enough to rest in who He has made you by your salvation in Him?

My Love,

I am perfectly at peace with you. I rest in us, and this is the ultimate test of a relationship. Can you trust me enough to rest in us and in what I am to you?

Be calm and relax in my contentment with you. You are exactly what I have always wanted and I am pleased with you.

I brought you into my palace, and even further than that,; I brought you into my chamber.
The entire dynamic of our relationship changed the very day you chose to accept my invitation.

Relax. Breathe deeply. Stop trying so hard to be 2good enough. Rest in me and what you are to me.

I love you and the timing of every one of your life events has opened your eyes to see me and has been absolutely perfect. Everything has been taken care of and there is nothing that has not been finished. Rest in us.

Yours Forever,
The King

Day 20

> *"The voice of my beloved! Behold, he cometh leaping upon the mountains, skipping upon the hills."*
>
> ### ~ Song of Solomon 2:8~
>
> The bride thrills at the sound of her king's voice. She loves the tones and pronunciation that he uses when he speaks to her. When you learn to identify God's voice in your life, the first thing you will notice is how much you love to hear Him speak.
> His voice is unlike any other and the more you hear it, the more you will understand that you will never want to go a day without it.

My Love,

I cannot wait to speak to you today. I love the way we communicate and I love the ease in which we talk to one another.

The way you tell me how much you love the sound of my voice will never get old to me. I cannot wait to speak to you and I am constantly looking for ways and opportunities to speak and express my heart to and for you.

You are my forever love and I will stop at nothing to exhaust creativity in expressing this to you.

Listen for my voice today in every place you go, everything that you do, and in everyone you meet. I am there and I am constantly speaking.

I speak in the wind which touches your face. My voice is in the sound of the leaves of the trees as they respond to my very breath.

My voice is in the laughter of a child and I am in the tears of the wounded soul. I can be heard in the prayer of the dying as well as in the first gasp of the newborn infant as he breathes his first taste of life.

I will never stop; I want you to learn to identify my voice in your very soul.

Keep speaking to me, my love. I cannot get over how my name sounds on your lips, and I will never get over the thrill of hearing your name pronounced on mine.

Desiring,
The King

Date _____

_____

_____

_____

_____

_____

_____

_____

_____

_____

_____

_____

_____

_____

_____

_____

_____

_____

Day 21

> *"My beloved is like a roe or a young hart: behold, he standeth behind our wall, he looketh forth at the windows, shewing himself through the lattice."*
>
> **~ Song of Solomon 2:9~**
>
> The bride is stirred by just a glimpse of the King through the lattice by her window. The lattice allowed her to catch a small glimpse of her beloved. The King of Kings allows you the opportunity to see little glimpses of Himself throughout your day, and it stirs you because you know that what you are able to see is only a small glimpse of something greater.

My Love,

I remember the very first time I ever saw you. You were completely unaware of me and really even of the fact I was watching you. Do you remember the first time you saw me?

It was magic, wasn't it? When our eyes met and you realized that I had been right in front of you all along, you were so completely overwhelmed when you identified me, you cried.

I love it when you look at me. I love it when you get in your car and scan the road ahead of you looking to see me, or when you walk into a crowd and whisper my name on your lips. I love seeing you look for me and I love how you ask me to show myself to you as you go about your day. I am always so close to you and I am constantly looking for ways to show my smile to you. I am never boring in this quest to get your attention. In fact, my love, I am shameless in my desire for you to see me.

I am in every song you hear and in the eyes of every individual you meet. I am in every conversation you have and every movie you watch. I am in the sunrise, sunset, ocean wave; you will hear me in every chirping bird above your head and every crunching leaf beneath your feet. You only need to speak my name and look with your eyes, intending to see me, and you will never be disappointed.

I love planning our times together; what you will discover during those times of togetherness is the forming of the world was just the tip of the iceberg in my creativity in the ways I can come up with for you to see me!

Look carefully today, because I cannot wait to lock eyes with you!

Always present
The King

Date _____

_____
_____
_____
_____
_____
_____
_____
_____
_____
_____
_____
_____
_____
_____
_____
_____
_____
_____

Day 22

> *"My beloved spake, and said unto me, Rise up, my love, my fair one, and come away."*
>
> **~ Song of Solomon 2:10~**
>
> The bride is speaking in this passage of what the king has said to her and his conversations with her always convey an invitation for relationship. The King of Kings desires for us to understand His voice, His methods of speaking, and His immense love for us.

My Love,

My heart has one cry that will forever resonate louder than any other and that cry is for us to be together.

Every time I speak, it will always be in reference to our relationship and how much I desire to communicate my love for you.

I will always take you to places where you can know me better, and I never want us to be apart in this journey. I called you to me and everything that I tell you is intentional.

Listen to me today. Memorize my pattern of speech with you. Examine the tones in which I address you. Learn to understand the name that I call you by, love, for it is unique to you and it conveys my dreams and intentions for you.

Do you remember the very first time you recognized my voice out of all the voices around you? Where were you? What was it that I said to you?

I love speaking to you and every time I speak, it is an invitation for us to be together and for you to learn my heart for you.

I desire you and I desire to speak that to you today!

All of my love,
The King

Day 23

"For, lo, the winter is past, the rain is over and gone; the flowers appear on the earth; the time of the singing of birds is come, and the voice of the turtle is heard in our land; the fig tree putteth forth her green figs, and the vines with the tender grapes give a good smell. Arise, my love, my fair one and come away."

~ Song of Solomon 2:11-13~

Solomon tells his bride that, now that the season has changed, there are places in the kingdom that he desires to show her. There are places in God's Kingdom He can only show us after we have endured specific seasons of life. Each season brings its own lessons of learning. Trust The King with your past seasons and allow Him to teach you the lessons that they contained.

My Love,

I know your heart has been wounded and so many have come and taken from you what they wanted or needed without a concern for the state of pain in which they left you. You do not look for a heart that is whole and flawless when you are looking for the perfect heart. You look for a heart that is scarred, bruised, and torn because this is a heart that has not been afraid to risk giving itself away. You have been misunderstood and treated in such a fashion that you may find these words difficult to take in or trust. I do not ask you to understand my heart for you just as you are at this moment, but I do ask you to simply accept my heart for you at this very moment. Draw close to me today and trust me with your scars and pain. I want to replace your fear and hurt with my confidence and my strength. You are beautiful to me beyond words, and our life together is made possible because of everything that has happened in the past.

Every dark moment, hurt, emotional wound, every feeling of despair that you have experienced has steered you to one empty well after another empty well until you stand here before me now.

It has all led you to me.
It has all led you home,
You are enough.

It is a new season for you, my love, and if you will take the time to
stop and listen, everything with which I have surrounded you will
point you to my power and my ability to see past your pain and focus
my love on your heart's repair. Every sound, color, voice, and
circumstance displays me.

My constant desire,
The King

Date _____

_____

_____

_____

_____

_____

_____

_____

_____

_____

_____

_____

_____

_____

_____

_____

Day 24

> *"O my dove, that art in the clefts of the rock, in the secret places of the stairs, let me see thy countenance, let me hear thy voice; for sweet is thy voice, and thy countenance is comely."*

~ Song of Solomon 2:14

Solomon was reassuring his bride she was in a place of safety. There are times when The King leads us to a place where we feel forgotten about. This is His place of rest and it is our security. Let Him move you in His time and do not try to open doors that He has not. Rest in the understanding that you are where He wants you and it is in this place of safety that He will hear your voice.

My Love,

I see your strength, but I also see just how delicate you are.

Retreat to me today. You have a gentle spirit within you and there are so many times you simply want to run away from the things and the people that cause hurt and conflict in your life.

When you received me, you gained an impenetrable fortress. You are safe with me. Let me cover you with my protection. I long to protect and to drive away any power which would seek to do you harm. Let me shelter and protect you today; and do not mistake my placing you in a place that seems to be out of the way of big opportunities for holding you back from what appears to be best. The walls are for your protection.

It is in the protective embrace of this place that I will teach you something that few people have the patience to learn - Who you are to me and who I am to you. It is here that I define our relationship. It is here in the stillness of this hideaway that I demonstrate my jealous protection of your heart.

Hide in me my love, and let me take your battles on as my own. We are one and I chose to make my stand with you.

I love you to no end.

All of my heart,
The King

Date _____

_____
_____
_____
_____
_____
_____
_____
_____
_____
_____
_____
_____
_____
_____
_____
_____
_____
_____
_____
_____
_____
_____
_____

Day 25

My Love,

I want you to know the potential you have is powerful! You have abilities within you to create beauty both in your life and in the lives of others your life touches.

There are people you will divinely meet today for the purpose of giving the words I place within your heart to them. I have been speaking to them in beyond audible ways; today you will deliver the audible message. A life can be changed with a single word, and today you have the potential to change lives, my love.

Hurts can be healed, mindsets that are lame can be made to walk, and blinded eyes can be opened and given sight. Prison doors of a heart can be opened, and the chains which so easily hold a life for years can be as easily broken with a single word. This is the potential that I see in you, my love; and this is the potential that you must guard so very carefully.

I have given you walls to protect your potential and I have given you the authority of my name to literally command that potential. Keep vigilant today against those little things that try to slip within the walls and sabotage everything that you are.

The "little foxes" can be a little word, a comment, or an un-authorized thought you accept as your identity. A word from another can wound and fester in your heart; and, if left undealt with, will cause decay and rot to your dreams. My love, understand today your purpose and your potential will bring others along who will seek to destroy it. Guard your heart, mind, will, and emotions today because these will be assaulted.

I love you and have waited for us to enjoy this relationship and for you to experience within yourself the realized potential that I have seen all along.

Living for you,
The King

Date _____

_____

_____

_____

_____

_____

_____

_____

_____

_____

_____

_____

_____

_____

_____

_____

_____

_____

_____

Day 26

> *"My beloved is mine, and I am his: he feedeth among the lillies."*
>
> ### ~ Song of Solomon 2:16
>
> What makes this passage so beautiful is the fact that the former shepherd girl is now in full understanding that she is now a queen. It is your understanding of what your relationship in Christ fully entails that ignites your purpose. You are His and He is yours and nothing can change that.

My Love,

You were made for me.

You breathed your first breath with the sole purpose of being mine. I have waited for you to find me, and every moment since your first until you discovered me I have been planning ways to convey my love for you.

You are mine from the top of your head to the tip of your toe and I belong to you. Never try to pretend to be anything other than yourself, my love, because you delight me!

Live in the understanding today that in spite of any of the "flaws" that you feel you possess, you are enough for me.

You are enough.

When it came to choosing, I chose you. I know every single thing about you and I chose you.

Never allow anyone to shake your understanding of this fact: *"my beloved is mine, and I am His."*

No matter what you do, where you go, or in what shape you may find yourself; you are mine. I am yours. I always have been and I always will be.

Having you makes me the richest King who ever has been.

Eternally yours,
The King

Date _____

_____

_____

_____

_____

_____

_____

_____

_____

_____

_____

_____

_____

_____

_____

_____

_____

_____

_____

_____

_____

_____

_____

Day 27

> *"Until the day break, and the shadows flee away, turn, my beloved, and be thou like a roe or a young hart upon the mountains of Bether."*
>
> **~ Song of Solomon 2:17~**
>
> In this passage the bride is pleading with her groom to let nothing get in the way of them being together. With God, there is no pleading necessary because nothing you could ever do would keep Him from you. There is nothing that you have ever done that has taken Him by surprise.

My Love,

So many times in this life you lose sight of just how big and expansive my power and love for you is.

You tend to focus on how "big" your offenses seem to be; and in doing so, you diminish how much bigger than your offense I truly am. I paid for your offenses on the cross. All of them.

This really has nothing to do with you, but rather it has everything to do with me. The search for you was messy, but I made it because you are worth getting messy for. I am not intimidated by your sin. I waded in over my head in humanity and its mess to bring you to me

I love you so much, and my love for you goes far deeper than any stain of sin could penetrate. You are mine now, and I will never let you go.

There is no mountain of doubt that you can create between us that I cannot or will not climb to bring this reminder to you. It can never be too steep or high to discourage me in any way. I have the power to climb any mountain you face. A man made mountain can be anything you allow to convince you I am distant or somehow blocked from you.

Even as you lie in the darkness of night, I watch you and I cannot turn my gaze away from you. You are so beautiful to me, my love.

You are so very real in your feelings and intents towards me. You captivate me with who you are. I am your beloved and you are mine. I will never stop reaching out to touch you and I will never stop climbing to be with you.

Love,
The King

Date _____

_____

_____

_____

_____

_____

_____

_____

_____

_____

_____

_____

_____

_____

_____

_____

_____

_____

_____

Day 28

> *"By night on my bed I sought him whom my soul loveth: I sought him, but I found him not."*
>
> ## ~ Song of Solomon 3:1~
>
> The bride looks for the king but will not find him until she is willing to leave her place of comfort. God is not always found where life is comfortable. Engaging Him often happens in places where we are not comfortable. Always be willing to leave what is familiar for what is true in your search for the King.

My Love,

My mind is forever on you.

One of my favorite times is being sought and then being found by you. I love this because I see how much it thrills you when the moment arrives that you realize we have connected.

Finding me does not happen for one who will never move past the desire to experience me. Finding me happens when you move past the desire to experience and into the actual effort of the search.

I am not always found in a place of comfort even though that is naturally where you would always hope to find me, nor am I always found on the timetable that you set for me to be found. Sometimes I can only be found in a place that is far beyond the borders of safety, comfort, and convenience. There are times when the search for me takes you places where you would naturally not desire to go. These places may seem difficult and even unsafe, but please know that if I have led you there, you are well protected.

No matter where that search takes you, I will be found by the one who is willing to do more than simply desire me from a platform of comfort.

Today I want you to be willing to look for me in the unexpected and the unplanned. I am there and I am waiting for you. This is the place where our relationship and your trust in me both deepen, and this is the place where you will always want to be.

Expectantly yours,
The King

Date _____

_____

_____

_____

_____

_____

_____

_____

_____

_____

_____

_____

_____

_____

_____

_____

_____

_____

_____

_____

_____

_____

_____

Day 29

> *"I will rise now, and go about the city in the streets, and in the broad ways I will seek him whom my soul loveth: I sought him, but I found him not."*

~Song of Solomon 3:2~

This passage is beautiful because the bride recounts her search for the king. Her search took her to multiple points of frustration, and a search which could have seemed like a waste now becomes something valuable to you. Your life's path may contain dead ends and back alleys but because of these events, you know all of the places where satisfaction was not. You have finally found Him and you can help direct those who are searching on where love can truly be found.

My Love,

Please do not stop looking for me.

There are three types of people in my kingdom. The first type will talk about me and listen to others talk about me. They love to talk and hear about me and they learn everything they can about me and about my kingdom through *listening*. They gather all of their facts with the exception of this being the only thing that matters. They will talk and even claim my rule over them but they will never truly seek me with their whole heart. They have no interest in ever really knowing me only in knowing about me.

The second desire to seek me but not enough to continue seeking after they reach what would appear to be a dead end. They get discouraged in their effort of the search and they simply decide to settle for never finding me.

I will not always be in the places or events that you think I should be found in. Just because a person has my name on his lips, his business card, or a sign out front, does not mean he ever had me in his heart.

A dead end in pursuit of me can be frustrating, but do not stop searching. Often I allow you to discover every empty well so that you can truly understand why it is that you are searching for me in the first place.

I can satisfy you.

I will not disappoint you or reject you, so please keep looking.

Today I want you to take a moment and mentally re-visit some of those empty wells that you came to in your pursuit of me. Re-visit in your mind all of those frustrating dead-end streets and wrong way commutes into which you invested your energy and heart.

You, without a doubt, know the names and final destinations of every street, passageway, well, and alley that did not lead you to me.

Today I want you to use this knowledge to help direct those that I place in your path. I want you to use what you have learned to help direct another past those streets and lead them to me.

Wrong way streets are never a waste of time and energy if you learn why it is that you went down them in the first place.

I am close enough to hear your thoughts. Keep searching!

The third type of person in my kingdom is rare. This type is the person who continues to search until he discovers that I have been with them all along.

You have never been alone.

Yours in everything,
The King

68

Day 30

"The watchmen that go about the city found me: to whom I said, saw ye him whom my soul loveth?"

~ Song of Solomon 3:3~

In this passage the shepherd girl is desperately searching for her love and her search led her to people, who by title, should have known where to find the King. Not everyone who carries the King's name is truly interested in The King or in building His Kingdom. In your search, do not settle for anything less than finding The King.

My Love,

When you look for me, the very first thing that you naturally want to do is go to another person for help in that search. You want to do this because it is easier than facing the struggles and hurts a search can bring. It feels safer to settle for something you do not want than risk hurt in achieving what seems to be difficult to achieve. I have made finding me in your life simple!

Don't settle!

I do use other people to speak and to help you, but I do not use everyone. Not everyone is going to be of a help to you in your search for relationship with me. Some will gravitate to you simply because you are searching and your willingness to search could be of a benefit to their own plans and agendas. But not everyone is going to be of help to you in hearing my voice or seeing my beyond-audible-touch.

Be mindful in your search and allow me to always direct you. Do not confuse any one person, thing, or event with the Source that you are seeking. The city has many watchmen in it, some by genuine calling and some by name and title alone. Some watch because of an inner desire to care for and to help protect those within the city walls of the kingdom. I have entrusted them with that desire and calling, while others watch for entirely different purposes -building their own kingdom within my kingdom. You will know them because their name is all over everything they do and the directions they give you in your search always lead you back to them. Do not confuse a watchman for the king.

I am your source. I am your relationship. I want to be everything to you. I can satisfy you.

Seek me and me alone today and let's enjoy each other to the fullest.

Always waiting,
The King

Date _____

_____
_____
_____
_____
_____
_____
_____
_____
_____
_____
_____
_____
_____
_____
_____
_____
_____
_____

Day 31

> *"It was but a little that I had passed from them, but I found him whom my soul loveth: I held him, and would not let him go until I had brought him into my mother's house, and into the chamber of her that conceived me."*
>
> **~ Song of Solomon 3:4~**
>
> The bride finds her King and has determined to never let him go. Once you truly experience God's love in your life, you will never be content with any other source. Do not feel that you are ever too much for God with your need for His attention. Run to Him with every need, concern, and care. He waits for your voice today.

My Love,

Be still. Stop moving for just a moment and understand that your search for me was not in vain. You have found me. Think about that for just a moment.

After every effort you have made in your search for me, you stand in my presence now because you have found me.

So stop every activity for just a moment and just listen and feel.

Sometimes the only way to hear my voice is to take a step away from every other voice in your life.

I do use other people to speak to you, into you, and over you; however I am perfectly capable of speaking directly to you and to you alone.

Today I want you to take the time to simply get quiet with the knowledge that you finally found me and that we are together. I also want you to think about the moment that you first saw me after your search. Do you remember what you did when you realized that it was really me you were looking at?

When you found me, you dropped everything else that you were holding on to in order to fully hold on to me. Empty your hands and your arms of everything that you have since picked up and fully hold me right now.

Drop all of your cares, worries, and the things that you so easily find yourself picking up along this journey. I love how you want me to be a part of everything that you are.

Don't ever let me go. You were made to hold me with everything that you have and I love the way you desire to fully embrace me in your life; you have discovered I am worth fully embracing.

Now that you have experienced the thrill of my embrace, you will never want to let go; you will not be satisfied until you have taken me into every personal place of your life.

An embrace is always amazing when it is mutually given and received; be still and feel my embrace in your soul. Enjoy the embrace and know that I have nothing in my arms but you. I love holding you and no matter what happens, I will never let you go.

Holding you forever,
The King

Day 32

> *"I charge you O ye daughters of Jerusalem, by the roes, and by the hinds of the field, that ye stir not up, nor awake my love, till he pleases."*
>
> **~ Song of Solomon 3:5~**
>
> What makes this passage so beautiful is that the bride is protective of her groom and seeks to do her best to make his comfort at the forefront of her attention. I believe it stirs the heart of God when we are protective of our relationship with Him. What lengths would you be willing to go to in order to protect your relationship with Him today?

My Love,

True love is determined by the extents and the lengths that you would go to in order to protect it.

I love how protective that you get about me, my name, and our relationship. I love how personal you take it and the way you bristle when a false word or misunderstanding is presented about me. You are so quick to defend me and that thrills me.

I am protective of you as well. When your name is brought up to me along with your faults, failures, and mistakes, the very first words out of my mouth are, "They are mine!"

You are mine. You have my name and I will always defend and protect you.

Thank you for loving me. Thank you for going to the lengths that you have to protect what you have in me. I am so glad to have you and I would not trade you or our relationship together for anything.

Today I want you to know that I would go to any extent to protect you and I will always go before you.

You are safe with me.

Everything is going to be alright.

Your Protector,
The King

Date _____

_____
_____
_____
_____
_____
_____
_____
_____
_____
_____
_____
_____
_____
_____
_____
_____
_____
_____

Day 33

> *"Who is this that cometh out of the wilderness like pillars of smoke, perfumed with Myrrh and frankincense, with all powders of the merchant?"*

~ Song of Solomon 3:6~

When the bride returns to her hometown she is no longer recognizable for the person that she once was. The differences in her stood out in a stark contrast to the person that she once was. You were created into a new creature at salvation and you now stand in a stark contrast to the person that you once were. The differences about you, because of Christ, now attract others to you. Do not be afraid to tell others who it was that changed you!

My Love,

I stand out. I always have and I always will. When you met me, I changed you. Our relationship has completely changed you.

There is no way that you can ever go back to what you were before we met.

People now notice you because our relationship has added to you.

The way you see things has changed. Your reason for smiling and for crying has even become radically different. What matters to you has changed along with what no longer matters.

Your search for identity no longer is found in what you want to become but has now become in the full realization of who you are.

People are drawn to the way the peace our relationship has added to your life stands in direct contrast to everything they know. Today I want you to understand that I made you to stand out. I made you to be seen and I made your spirit to be attractive to those around you. I did this the day that I made you mine. I love you and I love the ability that you have to reflect and radiate what our relationship has added to you.

I changed you. I made you royalty. I gave you my name, my favor, and my source of power because you were made to have those things.

Live your day with me and let's stand out and be noticed together. People want what we have!

Love,
The King

Date _____

_____
_____
_____
_____
_____
_____
_____
_____
_____
_____
_____
_____
_____
_____
_____
_____
_____
_____

Day 34

Solomon had sixty armed bodyguards that stood watch around his bed while he slept. They were unseen in the darkness by the bride, but she had knowledge of their presence. The darkness may hold unknown danger for you but the darkness also hides your ability to see your protection is watching over you. God is your protector and He is ever vigilant for your safety.

My Love,

You are safe with me. There will be times in which you will be afraid because of the darkness that seems to overwhelm you. The night conceals so much from you and this brings some measure of fear to you. Fear at any level is never from me.

The full understanding of my perfect love for you casts out fear. This knowledge throws back the suffocating cover of the unknown that seeks to strangle you in its paralyzing grip.

There is not one unknown that you will ever face that is not already fully understood and completely known to me.

The understanding and realization of my perfect love for you instills the ability and peace to perfectly trust; and while the darkness may conceal the details of the night to you, it often will conceal my protective covering with which I surround you.

My guard over you is never down and it is in a constant state of awareness.

I am more than able to defend you. Today I want you to know that along with any unknown that you may face, I have surrounded you with my protection as you go through this limited time of darkness. No condition is ever permanent and the darkness with all of its fear will only last for a little while. The dawn will always come.

Rest in me and in my promise to always protect and defend you. I value your life as my own.

Your protector,
The King

Date _____

_____

_____

_____

_____

_____

_____

_____

_____

_____

_____

_____

_____

_____

_____

_____

_____

_____

Day 35

> *"King Solomon made Himself a chariot of the wood of Lebanon. He made the pillars thereof of silver, the bottom thereof of gold, the covering of it purple, the midst thereof being paved with love, for the daughters of Jerusalem. "*

~ Song of Solomon 3:9-10~

Solomon built a chariot to bring his bride into his kingdom and it is an amazing picture of the work of Christ in us. The chariot was made from cedars of Lebanon which is what the cross of Calvary was made from. It is through the work of the cross that we are carried through the kingdom. The silver pillars picture His strength that holds us up, and the gold represents His mercy. We are covered by His royalty and surrounded by His love. The King Himself has built our chariot.

My Love,

You are not home yet. You belong with me and I have everything prepared for you when you finally arrive. Until then, there is the journey you make that brings us together. I want you to know I have provided and planned every moment of your journey. I have selected the route that you will be taking as well as the personally designed and built method of transportation that will bring you to me.

I have completely cared for every detail of your journey and step by step instructions have been laid out to guide you to the palace as you make your way to me through my kingdom. I know the terrain you must cross and I have carefully selected it just for you. I know the elements you will travel in and every person you will encounter on this journey. Nothing has been left to chance.

I have used the finest of materials for your transportation. You will be carried by my strength, and held up above the road by my mercy. You will be covered and protected from the threatening climate by my royalty. You will be completely surrounded by my love for you and no matter where your path takes you, you will arrive at my throne in complete rest.

Today I want you to trust that I am fully able and prepared to deliver you through any path that I have asked you to take. I have personally designed and built your method of transportation for this journey. Trust me as you travel and know that my love surrounds you. When the carriage comes to a stop and the door is opened for you, you step out onto the carriage steps, I will be waiting to take your hand and personally escort you into our palace where you will have your happily ever after.

Your protector
The King

Date _____

_____

_____

_____

_____

_____

Day 36

> *"Go forth, O ye daughters of Zion, and behold King Solomon with the crown wherewith his mother crowned him in the day of his espousals, and in the day of the gladness of his heart. "*
>
> **~ Song of Solomon 3:11~**
>
> There were two crowns that a king was given during the course of his reign. When he was ready to take a bride, his mother presented him with a crown of "espousals". This crown was constructed of vines and a plant material and it signified that he was deemed ready to take a bride. He was presented with a golden crown on the day of his wedding and this told those around him that he was determined worthy to rule. Jesus' crown of thorns signified the crown of espousals when he was shown worthy to take our transgressions and He will return again one day for His bride with a golden crown as our King of Kings.

My Love,

I have waited from the moment I first saw you to be the one you love.

I gave you the ability to give and receive love, and no other can love me the same way you can in your own unique and individual way. Your love and affection are completely unique; every gesture of adoration you present to me is valuable. I love your cry of dependency and the way you look up to me throughout your day to say thank you.

I went to where you were in order to meet you; when I laid eyes on you, I knew there would be no obstacle I would not overcome in order to make you mine.

I am relentless in my pursuit of you. I am fully able to claim you as mine. The events in your life have only served to bring you to me. I stand before you today and ask you to accept my unwavering and complete love for you. Take me and you take everything you will ever need. You will be taking completion to any void you may have in your heart and soul.

Today I stand here with my hand extended towards you inviting you to walk with me and allow me to show you how vast my kingdom truly is.

Today I ask you to walk in complete assurance of my acceptance of you.

Love,
The King

Date _____

_____

_____

_____

_____

_____

_____

_____

_____

_____

_____

_____

_____

_____

_____

_____

_____

_____

Day 37

> *"Behold, thou art fair, my love; behold, thou art fair; thou hast doves eyes within thy locks: thy hair is as a flock of goats, that appear on the mountain of Gilead."*

~ Song of Solomon 4:1~

In this passage Solomon is describing his bride and right from the start he mentions her hair. Goats were a sign of power in a kingdom in that day, and the sight of goats coming down a mountain slope was breathtaking because it symbolized the power of the owner. When Solomon looked at his bride it stirred his heart just as the heart of God is stirred when he sees us. We are an expression of His power to redeem and restore as only He can.

My Love,

I am overwhelmed whenever I look at you. The sight of your choosing to approach me is one I wish to capture as a permanent memory in my mind.

I study you. I notice every detail about you.

You look at yourself and you tend to get so focused and worried about things that are there that you feel shouldn't be and the things that are not there that you feel should be. Hear me now when I say that you are perfectly designed in every way.

I see you look in the mirror and I see the faces you make at the reflection you see and I smile.

I smile because I would not change a thing about what I see when I look at you. You are one of a kind, and you are my kind of beautiful.

Today I want you to be aware I do not make messed up or broken things. Everything I make is perfect and I only design priceless and precious gifts.

When you look at yourself today, please know I am looking at you as well and all I see is true and genuine beauty.

You have my attention,
The King

Date _____

_____
_____
_____
_____
_____
_____
_____
_____
_____
_____
_____
_____
_____
_____
_____
_____
_____
_____
_____
_____
_____
_____

Day 38

"Thy teeth are like a flock of sheep that are even shorn, which came up from the washing; whereof every one bear twins, and none is barren among them."

~Song of Solomon 4:2~

The King is expressing to his love how he anticipates her smile because he knows that he is the source of her grin. God loves your smile! The very source of our joy is Him. When you smile, you reflect Him to others and this is your greatest expression of The King that you can give.

My Love,

I love your smile.

I am captivated by it, and there is not one you have given I have not noticed. It is one of your most distracting features to me because the source of your smile is your heart.

I love knowing what it is that causes your heart to erupt in an uncontrollable smile and I desire to repeat this trigger because I cannot get enough of it.

I gave you your smile to reflect me and every time you give it away, it is one of the most powerful expressions of me you can give.

I cannot stop thinking about the way you grin. What have I done for you to make you smile today?

Was it the sunshine you felt on your skin, the flowers you saw in bloom, a newborn baby's giggle, a filling meal, clean sheets, fluffy bath towels, a delicious cup of coffee, children, grandchildren, or was it the fact I placed you on a person's mind to the point they called you?

Smile today because my heart leaps each time you do!

Love,
The King

Date _____

Day 39

> *"Thy lips are like a thread of scarlet, and thy speech is comely: thy temples are like a piece of pomegranate within thy locks."*
>
> **~ Song of Solomon 4:3~**
>
> The layer of skin on your temples is the thinnest layer of skin on your body. Your pulse is the most easily detected in your temples and when you are angry or emotionally stirred up. Your passion and the things which stir your heart are beautiful to God. Never be ashamed to take the way you feel to The King. He finds beauty in the expressions of your heart.

My Love,

I love how you speak out the words that your heart creates. You speak what matters most to you with passion and strength. It is beautiful to watch and even more so when you vocalize the words with which your heart creates to speak to me. The temple is the thinnest area of skin on the body and when your heart beats quickly, your pulse is clearly seen. How you feel matters to me.

When you are sad and you speak to me, I will stop at nothing to comfort you. When you are angry and confused, I will go to no end to teach you. When you are scared, I cannot help but demonstrate my strength; and when you are lonely I will be there to remind you I will never leave you.

Your expressiveness and your emotion is what provide you with beauty and when you emotionally express your heart to me, I am moved like no other time.

Don't hide your emotions from me and never feel ashamed about sharing your feelings about me because I long to teach you about my love for you. You are my forever love.

You have my attention,
The King

Day 40

> *"Thy neck is like the tower of David builded whereon there hang a thousand bucklers, all shields of mighty men."*
>
> **~ Song of Solomon 4:4~**
>
> King David had strategically built a tower, for his mighty men to barrack in, at the weakest place in his city's wall. The area around David's Tower became known as the safest place in the city. The people in its shadow knew that they were loved and valued by the king. Often times God will place you among the weakest of people in order to display His strength. Rest in the understanding of His awareness of your present location and plan in where He has placed you.

My Love,

I know your worth and it is, without a doubt, priceless because you are the only one of you that was ever made. I was there on the day you were first brought into existence and I know the purpose for which you were created. I know why you were designed and I have been patiently waiting until you were ready to learn this from me.

People can, at best, speculate your value, potential, and worth; and this speculation is based entirely upon what you are able to contribute to them. They can only see the surface of the unfinished structure and guess as to its purpose upon completion. They view the masterpiece as it is being painted and try to predict the final outcome of the artist's final brush strokes. They are not me.

I see everything from the first brush stroke to the result of the last. The tower of David was built to strengthen the weakest point in the city to provide strength. I have given you my strength and placed you among the weak so you can channel my strength to them. I have placed you strategically among people who need the strength you have found in me. Just as the tower was a symbol of security and strength to the people in its shadow, so you are a symbol of my love to them.

You carry this in your purpose so please do not be alarmed to discover you find yourself among the weak mindsets, aspirations, goals, and hearts of others.

Stand tall today, and walk in your purpose with a renewed understanding that you have the ability to direct people to The King! You are AMAZING, and I have always known it to be true and I see you growing daily into your purpose.

You have all of me,
The King

Date _____

_____
_____
_____
_____
_____
_____
_____
_____
_____
_____
_____
_____
_____
_____
_____
_____
_____
_____

Day 41

> *"Thy two breasts are like two young roes that are twins, which feed among the lilies."*

~ Song of Solomon 4:5~

Solomon is describing to his bride just how complete she is to him. She comes to him and he sees her as enough. You need to understand that this is how The King sees you. You are enough. You satisfy Him and He is more than enough to build up any area of our life in which we feel that we lack.

My Love,

You are complete in me. You feel as though you lack so much when you stand before me. I know why you feel this way and I want to help you with this. I want you to take time today to listen to what I am about to tell you. You are complete in me.

Complete means whole and without lack of anything. You are everything that I desire, and there is nothing you can ever do to change that. When you chose me and allowed yourself to be mine, I made up for any areas in which you had a lack or a need. I give you strength for weakness and beauty for ashes. I restore what was stolen from you and I mend what was broken. I heal your hurts and I calm your fears because that is my role in this relationship.

You satisfy me to no end in the fact that you are mine. I will never let you go and I will never leave you to fend for yourself. I am your protector and I jealously guard your heart and your feelings.

I am satisfied in our time together and I cannot wait to become everything to you. In time, as you learn who I am to you and who you are to me, you will see that my satisfaction in you is nothing that you can earn outside of who I am and what I have done for you.

You have all of me,
The King

Day 42

> *"Until the day break, and the shadows flee away, I will get me to the mountain of Myrrh, and to the hill of frankincense."*
>
> **~ Song of Solomon 4:6~**
>
> Solomon wanted his love to start her day with the full knowledge of just who she was to him. In the stillness of the morning, just before you rise for the day, take a moment to think about the fact that God truly does love you and that you have been made righteous in Him. You are second to none. You are His beloved and nothing will ever change this fact.

My Love,

Don't move another inch until I tell you what is on my heart.

The quietness and the stillness of the dawn will not last and soon you must start your day. Before you do, take a moment to think about the fact that you have been fully and wholly forgiven and redeemed. Your place with me was guaranteed through the sacrifice of another and your future has been secured because of a resurrection.

You were meant to be with me and you were meant to fully enjoy me. Let me love you and let me be your source for security. There is nothing that can separate you from me and there is nothing that could ever cause me to love you any less. You owe me nothing because I have given everything that I am to you out of love.

Inhale me, and the fragrance of my heart and love for you will deaden the pain of anything that you are going through. Inhale my fragrance of love, forgiveness, truth and life. Breathe me in and allow this knowledge to fill you so that you can exhale me to others.

You are righteous, you are royalty, and most importantly of all, you are mine!

Yours,
The King

Day 43

> "Thou art all fair, my love; there is no spot in thee."
>
> **~ Song of Solomon 4:7**

My Love,

There are so many voices calling for your attention today and only one of which you need to focus everything you have on. Mine.

Each time you listen to me you will be invited to operate from my love for you and never for it. You never need to try to do anything to earn my love for you and there is nothing you can do that will cause me to love you more than I already do.

You are perfect to me. There are many people who will tell you all of the things about yourself that you need to change in order to please me. People that know of me are different than those who actually know me personally. If you truly know me then you know that it is the actions of the cross that guaranteed my pleasure, not your effort for improvement. You will be approached by people who have so many ideas of what they think will make me happy, but there is only one thing that you can do to truly please me.

Believe.

Believe me when I tell you are who and what I made you to be. Believe I am who I say I am and that I have done what I said I have done. Do not base your identity on how you feel about yourself or what others say you should or should not do. If you ever need to know what I want changed about you, just ask me! I will tell you what it is you need to know about you and me.

You are righteous. You are set apart, and there is NO fault in you!

Yours,
The King

Day 44

> *"Come with me from Lebanon, my spouse, with me from Lebanon: look from the top of Amana, from the top of Shenir and Hermon, from the lions' dens, from the mountains of the Leopards."*

~ Song of Solomon 4:8~

In this passage, Solomon not only informs his bride there are sights in the kingdom he wants her to see, but that he wants to be with her when she sees these sights. The King is inviting you to experience His kingdom with Him today. He wants you to be aware of His constant presence and to understand there is nothing in your life left up to chance. He has personally planned every opportunity you will see today.

My Love,

Abide in me today!

This day is brand new and with it will come brand new opportunities for us to be together.

I cannot wait to take you with me in every place that I desire to go. I want you to go with me because my journeys and appointments would not be as enjoyable without you. There is so much that I want you to see because in seeing those things, you will further learn who I am to you.

I want to take you places that you, in the past, have stayed away from because of fear. You need not entertain a fear of heights because I will be climbing with you. Today I want us to climb together to a place where you can view just how expansive and powerful I am. This is a major key in your journey, because I belong to you. Completely and wholly I am yours, and this view is crucial to your understanding of just how valuable you are in my world.

I could simply tell you all of this but I long to show you in ways you can see to help you comprehend. I know you and I know that sometimes you need to see to believe.

I know how to communicate to you, so let go of your fear and operate in the knowledge of my love for you and my protective nature over what and who belongs to me. Clear your agendas and plans and let me take you to places where I can show you my power. Decide right now to enjoy the view and the journey as we climb together.

Relax, because I have the entire day planned!

Eternally yours,
The King

Date _____

_____

_____

_____

_____

_____

_____

_____

_____

_____

_____

_____

_____

_____

_____

_____

_____

_____

Day 45

> *"Thou hast ravished my heart, my sister; thou hast ravished my heart with one of thine eyes, with one chain of thy neck."*
>
> **~ Song of Solomon 4:9~**
>
> Solomon mentions the eyes of his bride frequently. He loved looking into her eyes because when he did, he was fully aware of the fact she was looking back at him. Do not hide your eyes from God. When you take the time to look for Him in your day to day activities, you cannot help but be aware of His gaze back at you. Look for Him and to Him today and cherish the fact of His awareness of you.

My Love,

You have my heart completely.

You were designed to see beauty and be moved by it to your very core. Your eyes are directed, by your mind, to take in the things you wish to know more about. This is how you're made to learn, and because of this, your gaze is one of your most powerful expressions of love to me.

When you are confronted with something that repulses you or loses your interest, you turn your gaze away. This is what makes your eyes so powerful to me. The choice to look at me over all of the sideshows and distractions that call out for your attention, an action that seems to be so simple, launches my heart into overload. You capture my heart and it pulls at every fiber of my being when you seek to see me throughout your day.

As life brings your greatest need, look at me.

Should you find yourself in a season of deepest hurt, fix your gaze on mine.

The connection of our gaze will remind you of two truths that often get lost in the events of time. The first truth is when your eyes find mine, you will see I have been waiting for your glance. The second truth you will see is just how much I am aware of everything you face. I will not run and I will not hide from you, no matter where you are when you choose to look at me because it was that place in your life that caused you to look to me. I will strengthen you and we will overcome any difficulty together.

I am yours and everything I am belongs to you because I made you mine. I love you and will do so forever!

Captivated,
The King

Date _____

_____

_____

_____

_____

_____

_____

_____

_____

_____

_____

_____

_____

_____

_____

_____

_____

_____

Day 46

> *"How fair is thy love, my sister, my spouse! How much better is thy love than wine! And the smell of thine ointments than all the spices."*
>
> ### ~ Song of Solomon 4:10~
>
> King Solomon cherished the love of this shepherd girl because she willingly gave her heart to him. Her love was without a selfish motive of expected return. He had disguised himself as a shepherd when he met her, and she was completely unaware of his royalty. When she discovered his true identity, she felt undeserving and unable to be worthy of his attention. You feel this way when you compare your level love for Him to His level of love for you. It was never designed to be equal. He is The King and He chose you. What stirs His heart about your love is that you chose to extend it to Him. You satisfy Him.

My Love,

You are enough. There are days when I know you think about the measure of love you give to me and you compare it to the measure of love I give to you and it makes you feel as though you are not enough. I want to correct that thinking because our measures of love were never designed to be equal.

I do not want a checklist of actions or services you perform for me in order to prove to me that you love me. A checklist is only used to remind a person to do something; love is not something you are to be reminded to give.

No, what makes your love spectacular to me and what sets you apart from the "checklist" crowd is that you give your love to me by choice. You choose to love me and a heart that is given, in the end, is in fact a heart given.

I love that you chose to give me your heart even though you get sad when you look around at others who seem to have more to give than you. You still hold up your heart to me and your heart is all that I have ever wanted. Money cannot truly buy a heart and temporal sources used to trade for a surface feeling will quickly fade away into a cold winter of the soul. But love that is purposefully given is rare and priceless.

Today, at some point in time, I want you to look in the mirror and remind yourself that you are enough for me. Live today *from* my love and never again *for* my love. You are and will always be enough for me.

Satisfied,
The King

Date _____

_____
_____
_____
_____
_____
_____
_____
_____
_____
_____
_____
_____
_____
_____
_____
_____
_____
_____
_____

Day 47

> *"Thy lips, O my spouse, drop as the honeycomb: honey and milk are under thy tongue; and the smell of thy garments is like the smell of Lebanon."*
>
> ### ~ Song of Solomon 4:11~
>
> God loves your voice. He made it unique and today is the day to just speak to Him. Sing to Him. Speak of Him to others around you. He gave your voice with its individual tones and inflections and He loves when you use it to touch Him. What has The King done for you within the last sixteen hours? Today you need to tell someone why you love Him so much and why you are glad that He found you when He did.

My Love,

I love the way you speak to me.

Today I want you to do something very different. Over the last forty six days, I have written to you and encouraged you to write your feelings back to me based upon what each day has revealed to you about your understanding of where you stand with me.

Today I want you to not write your thoughts about me on paper, but rather I want you to speak them to me. I inhabit your praise. Speak my name and tell me how you feel about me.

I love the way your heart transposes your innermost thoughts and then relays them through your voice. All of nature praises me because I command them to praise me, but you are unlike all of nature. I made you with the choice to praise me. I wish that you could hear for just a moment what nature in its entirety sounds like when it speaks my praise. It is like an overwhelming symphony.

The one instrument that I desire is the one that plays, not by command, but by choice. Speak to me today.

What is on your heart? What would you say to me if I were there right in front of your eyes in a way that you could see me? What do you want me to know?

Your lips have said so many things since the day that you were born and yet I anticipate each moment that you speak my name. You are remarkable, special, brilliant, kind and an ultimate reflection of me. Speak to me!

Always yours,
The King

Day 48

> *"A garden enclosed is my sister, my spouse; a spring shut up, a fountain sealed."*
>
> **~Song of Solomon 4:12~**
>
> Solomon had a garden that was reserved for him alone. In the garden was a fountain that was sealed with his signet ring and no one in the kingdom could touch that fountain. He was letting his bride know that she was his. Scripture states you are sealed until the day of redemption. You belong to The King for His exclusive use and are protected from any power that would seek to harm you. He enjoys who you are as a person and you delight Him!

My Love,

You are mine and I cannot begin to tell you how much that thrills me.

I love your attention. One of my favorite times with you is when you just stop whatever you are doing and focus on me. It is during these times that I am best able to communicate how much my mind and my heart are focused on you.

Look for me. Listen for my voice. Stop moving for just a moment and breathe deeply. Deep within your spirit I am speaking. My peace is yours and I will jealously fight to protect you from any source that seeks your harm. You belong to me and I am never apart from you.

Like a private fountain, sealed by the King's signet ring for his use alone, I have sealed you for me.

I enjoy you! I anticipate our time together and nothing can ever change my heart toward you.

The cost to bring us together is minimal in comparison to the value that our relationship brings to me and that your presence has brought to the kingdom.

Today I want you to simply enjoy the attention that I give to you. I will go before you and open doors that you thought could never be opened. Let yourself enjoy our kingdom. It was made for you.

All of my heart,
The King

Date _____

_____

_____

_____

_____

_____

_____

_____

_____

_____

_____

_____

_____

_____

_____

_____

_____

_____

Day 49

> *"Thy plants are an orchard of pomegranates, with pleasant fruits; camphire with spikenard and saffron; calmus and cinnamon, with all trees of frankincense; myrrh and aloes, with all the chief spices: a fountain of gardens, a well of living waters, and streams of living waters, and streams from Lebanon."*
>
> **~Song of Solomon 4:13-15~**
>
> The garden of Solomon was a feat of incredible power because he had it created in a wasteland. He irrigated it and planted thousands of different plants and trees in an environment where they would never have naturally been found. When Solomon viewed this garden, he was reminded of his power. God planted you from your natural environment in a place where you would not have naturally flourished. His Spirit nourishes you and you bloom from His life. You remind Him daily of His power in your very presence before Him.

My Love,

Everything about you pleases me. I see you through what I did to bring you to me, and into this relationship.

I look at you and I immediately sense satisfaction in my heart because I am satisfied with you.
You are beautiful and fragrant to me because you remind me, simply by your presence, that I am powerful. I took you from where you were and planted you here forever with me.

You are fragrant and you are absolutely stunning to behold where you now stand; no one else could have transplanted you to the place where you now grow. No one else could have made you grow in a place so very different than your natural environment.

You possess me and now possess healing, peace, strength, nourishment, and every good thing. You bloom and everyone who passes by you notices your color and your richness. You are my perfect garden, and I cannot get enough of you.

Today I want you to walk in the fact I am pleased with you and I enjoy your company beyond any other. You are mine and I love that!

Love,
The King

Date _____

_____

_____

_____

_____

_____

_____

_____

_____

_____

_____

_____

_____

_____

_____

_____

_____

_____

_____

_____

Day 50

> *"Awake, O north wind; and come, thou south; blow upon my garden, that the spices thereof may flow out. Let my beloved come into his garden and eat his pleasant fruits."*
>
> **~Song of Solomon 4:16**
>
> God designs events in our life in order to awaken us to His presence. Your life events have served to bring you into an awareness of Him. Never discount or look back on the events of your life as a waste because it is those events that have brought you into your awareness of His hand in your life.

My Love,

I want you to be awake with me today. So many people will live out their entire life asleep to me and to every opportunity that I make available to them. I have so much to give you of me today. I have creatively prepared so much for you to see and experience; and, if you could fully see it, you would live your life in constant and total amazement. Your attention to me stirs me and the more it stirs me, the more I want to flourish and bloom for you on a daily, hourly, and moment by moment basis.

Open your heart to me today. Look for me in everything that you see around you. Ask the right questions and out of everything you see and everything you do. Ask me to display my love and voice to you today. I am ready right now to show you everything about yourself that is strength and beauty. You can bloom because of your relationship with me.

You have so much potential and you have an abundance of possibilities to offer those that surround you. Let my attention for you stir you, and let your learning of all that I have to offer you in turn teach you how to offer your potential to others. You are my garden, and I made you to be seen.

Love,
The King

Day 51

> *"I am come into my garden, my sister, my spouse: I have gathered my myrrh with my spice; I have eaten my honeycomb with my honey; I have drunk my wine with my milk: eat, o friends; drink, yea, drink abundantly, o beloved."*
>
> **~Song of Solomon 5:1~**
>
> Solomon compares his bride to this incredibly beautiful and protected place in his kingdom. It is a place that he compares her to many times in his song. The message for you is that God made you incredible and special in His sight. You are anything but common to Him and you are protected and desired. He compares you with the most tender and beautiful of His creations and has you strategically placed where everyone can see how beautiful that you are.

My Love,

I want you to be with me, so that you can in turn show others what this relationship that we share can do for a life.

I protect you with walls that no one could ever break and I nurture your very spirit with my own. I provide for you and enjoy every moment that we spend together. Your heart is all that I want. I know that your life's choices call for your attention, and I wait patiently. You may play hard to get sometimes, but I will never give up pursuing you. You will have to fight to not love me in return.

I move on your life and in your spirit for one purpose; to see my Spirit flow forth out of you. You are a living extension of me and the source that satisfies you is also enough to satisfy their thirst. You have within you what they need to find comfort, love, forgiveness, patience, temperance, joy, longsuffering and peace. You wear the scent of all of these fruits and they are valuable to those around you.

Open your heart to me today.

Invite me into your life to tend the garden that I have planted .Trust me to care for you in every situation and hold no area back from me.

I made you for me to care for and to enjoy. You are my garden and I will fight for you jealously.

You have been sealed for my purpose alone. Rest in the fact that my seal is upon you and that I have chosen you!

Love,
The King

Date _____

_____
_____
_____
_____
_____
_____
_____
_____
_____
_____
_____
_____
_____
_____
_____
_____
_____
_____
_____

Day 52

> *"I sleep, but my heart waketh: it is the voice of my beloved that knocketh, saying, open to me, my sister, my love, my dove, my undefiled: for my head is filled with the drops of the night."*
>
> **~Song of Solomon 5:2~**
>
> Never pass on the opportunity to experience more of God. Anytime that God knocks on your hearts door you will be faced with the decision to open the door or excuse away the opportunity. Always choose to move with Him over being comfortable.

My Love,

Never pass on the opportunity to open your heart's door to experience more of me.

So many times people choose to sleep while I am trying to speak to them. Carelessness slights my attention. The door is always a picture of an opportunity to share more of me. There is the unknown beyond the door, and unknown will always be a platform for faith; I call you to experience the unknown with me. It is the places that appear to be the most insecure that I invite you to experience because it is in those places where your reliance in me grows.

I will always invite you to choose being awake with me over a life and attitude of sleep. There is so much for you to see and to experience.

Do not pretend to have only a little strength when I knock, and please choose me over the comforts of where you rest. My grace is shown by the very sound of my hand on your door.

Always choose to leave what is comfortable and familiar for what is true. Always choose me over every other option, even those that would seem to make more sense. Stay awake with me today. Life is easy with your eyes closed, but it is far more rewarding if you keep your eyes open.

Open your eyes and your heart to see my hand in your life. Let's be awake together today.

Always inviting,
The King

Date _____

_____

_____

_____

_____

_____

_____

_____

_____

_____

_____

_____

_____

_____

_____

_____

_____

_____

_____

_____

_____

_____

Day 53

> *"I have put off my coat; how shall I put it on? I have washed my feet; how shall I defile them?"*
>
> **~Song of Solomon 5:3~**
>
> The bride faced a choice here of comfort over relationship. In the moment of decision, she did what so many of us do and that is to excuse away the opportunity. Moving with God is the single most adventurous thing that you can do!

My Love,

I want you to have everything you need, and I provide for anything your heart desires of me. I only ask that you not choose comfort over your relationship with me.

It is very easy to become distracted by everything you have and lose sight of what it is you need. When I call, do not let anything prevent you from moving in the direction I call you. Do not let anything become an excuse that would cause you to ignore the presence of our relationship.

Today I want you to evaluate where you are in me and where you are in this relationship. Ask the hard questions of yourself and ask me to remind you of where you stand in my heart. The answer that I give you is what I want you to keep in the forefront of your mind when the "knock" comes in your life. I am constantly seeking to open your eyes to my vastness and in the area of my love for you. Be ready to move in that love and be ready to open the door anytime you hear me knock.

Look for me today. I am big enough to get past any distractions that may cross your path today. There is nothing that can keep me from you, but there are things you can allow to keep you from enjoying all of me. Nothing is worth losing sight of all the benefits this relationship entitles you. Walking with me is the most adventurous activity you could ever do and the things that you will see, experience, and learn by walking with me will be far greater than any temporary comforts you could gain by making an excuse to not walk with me at my invitation.

Listen for me to today. Be aware of me and my presence.

Lovingly yours,
The King

Date _____

_____

_____
_____
_____
_____
_____
_____
_____
_____
_____
_____
_____
_____
_____
_____
_____
_____
_____

Day 54

> *"My beloved put in his hand by the hole of the door, and my bowels were moved for him. I rose up to open to my beloved, and my hands dropped with myrrh, and my fingers with sweet smelling myrrh, upon the handles of the lock."*
>
> ### ~Song of Solomon 5:4-5~
>
> When the bride saw the king move, it stirred her to her core. Seeing God move always stirs our heart because we know His knock on our heart's door is always a call to a greater level of relationship. The brides direct response was to move to answer. This is our greatest and most rewarding response to His call.

My Love,

When you see me move in your life it stirs your desire for me in an amazing way.

I am very present in your life and I surround, with my presence, the very circumstances you feel overwhelm you. There is nothing about you or your life that escapes my attention. I protect you.

Today I want you to rest in me. Rest in my awareness of you and let me go before you and move in your day. Trust me to open and close doors, and watch me move for your good. The seasons of your life that seem difficult to understand are for a purpose. My "knock" on your heart's door sometimes comes in a form that sounds like heartbreak, financial or medical setback. It is not an unfair move on my part, but rather a "knock" on your hearts door. It is an invitation, my love.

I am always inviting you to a closer relationship in everything I allow on your path. Do not miss the opportunity because you mistake the "knock" for an unfair circumstance. Open the door and ask me to find more of me in whatever form the "knock" has taken. I am waiting to show you more about me.

When you remove any hesitation to allow me access you will see me move in your life in an unbelievable way. The response from you to my working in your life will always be a deeper love from you to me. You are moved by my presence in your life, and I am moved by your presence in mine.

You have my love,
The King

Date _____

_____
_____
_____
_____
_____
_____
_____
_____
_____
_____
_____
_____
_____
_____
_____
_____
_____
_____

Day 55

> *"I opened to my beloved; but my beloved had withdrawn himself, and was gone: my soul failed when he spake: I sought him, but I could not find him; I called him, but he gave me no answer."*

~Song of Solomon 5:6~

The bride must have felt such disappointment when the door was opened and the groom was gone. Sometimes The King seems absent but you can be assured that He is always aware of you. There are times you will feel alone, however; during these times you must hold tightly to what you know about who God is and who you are to Him. He holds you!

My Love,

You must learn one thing about me above all else. I am always aware of you. There are times when you will look for me in your circumstance and I appear to be silent. You may have even been calling out to me even now and your very soul seems to faint within you at my lack of response. You have searched for me and I seem to be non-existent.

I am here and I am very much aware of you and everything that you are going through. Please do not confuse my lack of your specifically expected answer for help with my absence. There are times where you desire my response to your situation to align with your ideas of what that response should be.

My ways are higher than your ways and my thoughts are higher than your thoughts. I protect you and I guard your steps jealously. I will never leave you to fend for yourself, and the day I took you in is the day you were forever given my care. There is nothing that can separate you from me. In the times where you cannot seem to see my hand, trust my heart. Know these things I have promised to you and know that I never break my promises. You are mine and I am yours.

Your confidence,
The King

Day 56

> *"The watchmen that went about the city found me, they smote me, they wounded me; the keepers of the walls took away my veil from me."*
>
> **~Song of Solomon 5:7~**
>
> The bride's veil was a symbol of her identity as a queen. It represented her relationship to him and I find it interesting that the guards sought to take this from her. You will find people on your path who will try to convince you that you are not who God says that you are to Him and they may even seek to take from you the very things that you feel identify you with Him. You are His and no one can take you from His complete love and acceptance for you.

My Love,

One of the most difficult things to learn to accept and understand is that not everyone wants you to find The King.

This is especially difficult to comprehend when it comes to people who would appear to be a part of my kingdom, but the fact remains, not everyone is interested in aiding your search for me. People, sometimes even the well-meaning, can lose focus on their purpose and become territorial. They take their eyes off of my value and operate out of their own resources to achieve significance and value in the adoration and approval of others. This can cause them to strike out at someone who is in their search for me; someone like you.

This can especially be true to those who, by title, are supposed to be able to direct others to me. The watchmen are supposed to know where I am and be able to direct those looking for me in the right direction. They can wound the most harshly at times. There are some who will seek to take away from you the very things that identify you as mine. The veil is a symbol of union. It is a picture of your royalty; it is not royalty in itself. There are people who will seek to take away the things from you that give you your identity and freedom in me. They will try to substitute it with programs, agendas, plans, and ideas of their own.

Royalty was given to you by me, and it is something that can never be taken away from you. Walk in confidence of who you are in me today and forgive those who have sought to keep you from me. The wounds you received from them have clearly shown who they are, and this alone is invaluable in your search for me. I love you and cannot wait for you to see me in your life today!

Yours forever,
The King

Date _____

_____

_____

_____

_____

_____

_____

_____

_____

_____

_____

_____

_____

_____

_____

_____

_____

_____

_____

_____

_____

Day 57

God loves it when we speak of Him to others. The bride was expressing her love of her king to those around her and was overcome with emotions when she thought of what he meant to her. Thinking about God will always produce thankfulness for God. The reaction to thankfulness will always be praise, and praise leads to action. Take time to meditate on what The King has done in your life, and let the results of thinking flow from your life today.

My Love,

I love how you speak of me to those around you.

You always seem to find a way to introduce me into every conversation. There is always something I have shown you that relates to what is happening in the moments of engagement you have with others. You share the things I show you and the ways I speak to you so beautifully.

Your desire is shown through the things that captivate your conversation because what is in your heart will always dominate what you choose to discuss with others.

When someone is hurting, you seek to comfort them with me as your first response. When someone feels discouraged and lonely, you are so quick to tell them about my care. When weakness is expressed to you I love how you unfailingly tell of my strength.

It is not the speaking of me to others that is so overwhelming, but rather it is what the speaking of me does to your heart that gets me each and every time. Your heart desires more of me.

When you speak to others of my love for you, you express me in such a magnificent way and you conduit who I am to those around you.

So many people have been made to believe they are not worth receiving love or that they are incapable of having what I have given to you. This is a lie. I am the truth and you have been made free to share that truth.

Share me with someone else today. Freely give the love I have so freely given to you.

Yours forever,
The King

Date _____

_____
_____
_____
_____
_____
_____
_____
_____
_____
_____
_____
_____
_____
_____
_____
_____
_____
_____

Day 58

> *"What is thy beloved more than another beloved, O thou fairest among women? What is thy beloved more than another beloved that thou dost so charge us?"*
> ### ~Song of Solomon 5:9~
>
> People want to know what makes your God so great. They want to know why it is you cling to Him so tightly and how you gain strength and comfort from Him. Answer them today. Speak of my goodness to you and show them how I have added to your life.

My Love,

I love the way you look for me and how you desire to be close to me.

Your desire for me shows in the way you speak about me. You defend me if I am being misrepresented. You are fiercely loyal to me and you seek to protect me like no other. You want people to understand and know me. You even hurt inside when they do not.

They want to know how you can remain firm and calm in the middle of a crisis and how you are able to stand without fear for what is right. They want to know how you can provide so much strength for others in your times of loss. They see glimpses of me in you, and although it may appear to cause some to avoid you, it causes all to wonder what it is you have in this relationship with me.

Today I want you to tell them:

Tell them of the love I have for you and tell them how you see this love demonstrated. Brag on me. So many people are empty and simply want a real relationship. They cover it up in so many ways, but every time they are around you they are asking, what makes the relationship we have so special. Tell them today!

Forever yours,
The King

Day 59

> *"My beloved is white and ruddy, the chiefest among ten thousand."*
>
> **~Song of Solomon 5:10~**
>
> The word white used here to describe King Solomon is not a color white but rather a word that means 'brilliantly clear'. There is nothing murky or unclear about how God feels about you, and this is what sets Him apart from the other relationships in your life. He desires for you to know everything about Him and will never hide any part of His heart from you.

My Love,

I want you to know me as well as you know yourself. I love your desire to notice every detail about me. I love the way you describe me to others because one of the very first things you tell people is what it was about me that captured your attention.

My heart for you is transparent and clear. I know everything about you and I know everything you have ever done. I know the reason you had behind every course of action you have ever taken. I know every smile of achievement you have given as well as every downward glance of shame. I know what makes you cry and feel sad and I know the things that bring you the sweetest times of happiness.

In the perfect understanding of everything that is you, I love you and would choose you over and over again. You are everything to me, my love.

I know what it is like to have been hurt, wronged and taken advantage of. I know what it is like to empty yourself for another without being noticed or even to be misunderstood and rejected. I am taken with you and am so glad you are mine. I complete you in the most amazing ways.

Yours with no end,
The King

Day 60

> *"His head is of the most fine gold, his locks are bushy, and black as a raven."*
>
> **~Song of Solomon 5:11~**
>
> There is a tremendous amount of symbolism in this passage. The gold mentioned here speaks of purity and the head is speaking of purpose and mind. The mind is the power box of our actions, so this passage tells us his thoughts for us are pure and filled with purpose. The dark hair symbolizes strength. His thoughts and actions are framed in by His strength to carry out the actions produced by His thoughts.

My Love,

There has been so many times I have called you to take your focus off of the things, circumstances, and people around you and focus solely on me. This request has been by design. When you take your eyes off yourself, you place them upon me.

When you look at me, my love, you will see everything you would have missed if you were not looking at me. You will see the clarity of purpose I have given your life, and you will see that I am trustworthy.

There is nothing murky or muddy about me. I am brilliantly clear in my plans and desires for you. When you look at me, you will see my thoughts for you are pure and right. I desire the very best for you and will take you on the most complexly creative journey in accomplishing within you what I made for you to enjoy with me.

When your gaze looks to me, you will see my strength all around you. It frames you completely and there is nothing you will ever have to do to achieve it. I give you my strength, and I will exhaust every avenue I possess to show this to you.

Today you are going to be given the same choice you are given every day. Today I want you to be very aware of this choice. You will decide between looking around you at all of the noise, distractions, words of others, or the actions for and against you; and you can decide your identity comes from these sources or you can look at me. You can see me for who I am in you today, and you can choose to draw your identity from me. Choose me.

Your forever love,
The King

Date _____

_____

_____

_____

_____

_____

_____

_____

_____

_____

_____

_____

_____

_____

_____

_____

_____

_____

Day 61

> *"His eyes are as the eyes of doves by the rivers of waters, washed with milk, and fitly set."*
>
> ### ~Song of Solomon 5:12~
>
> The bride describes Solomon's eyes and compares them to the most peaceful and gentle creatures she can think of. When you take the time to truly look into God's eyes, you will see, His eyes are completely focused on you. His eyes are clear, focused, observant, and they declare peace.

My Love,

When you take the time to look into my eyes there is something that will always stand out to you. Once you see it, you will never be able to escape from its constant reality.

My eyes are completely focused on you. This is something that will never change no matter where you go or what you do. I will forever be watching out for you. I see your frustrations and your pains. Every time you feel completely abandoned, know that I am here as a constant. My gaze is clear and precise. I see you with the intention of helping you in every circumstance you face. There is no detail about what you face that escapes my attention.

You will see my eyes radiate peace. I am at peace with you. The day I brought you into a relationship with me was the day that I declared a permanent peace with you. This peace is based entirely upon me and it can never change.

You will see that my eyes hold you in extreme value. They are clear and open for I have nothing to hide from you. I want you to know my heart for you. Today I ask you to take a moment to quiet yourself and look up. When you see all of the sky above you, know I am at looking right back at you. My eyes are set on you as they always have been and always will be.

Eyes on you,
The King

Day 62

My Love,

I want you to think about what it would be like to walk into a room filled to capacity with spices. Spices like oregano, garlic, and basil. It would be completely overwhelming to your senses, and there is no way that you could walk into such a room and be unaffected.

When you think of my cheeks, you must see the face of Jesus. I want you for just a moment to take into your mind the image of my Son and what He did in order to bring you to me. They were beaten until they were unrecognizable. They were bloodied and torn open, but the words that came from His lips were every bit as healing as myrrh. Do you remember what He said?

"Father, forgive them, for they know not what they do."

Forgiven.

Myrrh is only extracted from its producing tree through viciously beating the trunk to the point that it bleeds out its precious healing substance. You gather myrrh to use it as an antiseptic for blood issues. When you think of the healing effect that the words of Christ held for your blood's inadequacy you can see how beautiful my cheeks are. The image is as overwhelming to the senses as spices and yet as beautiful and breathtakingly sweet as the flowers in a garden.

Take in the thoughts of what Jesus has done for you and meditate on the fact that He was wounded for your transgression and by His stripes, you were spiritually healed forever. Christ left His place in the heavenly palace so that you never have to leave yours.

Always for you,
The King

135

Day 63

> *"His hands are as gold rings set with the beryl: his belly is as bright ivory overlaid with sapphires."*

~Song of Solomon 5:14~

The bride is describing the hands of her groom, and notice the words that she uses to describe them. She describes them like a ring, which is a picture of strength; and then she speaks of an inlay which symbolizes a delicate nature to his touch. She mentions his belly being made of ivory which is a very beautiful but fragile material. This is a beautiful picture of God. His hands are strong enough to defend us yet tender enough to repair even the most delicate of hurts. The word compassion comes from the Greek work meaning stomach. Christ is easily broken with compassion for our hurts and trials and in this I see the ivory beautifully pictured.

My Love,

When you think about my hands, what do you think they look like? How would you describe my hands to another person?

My hands are strong. My hands are steady and experienced. My hands are safe and can hold so much. They are hands you can trust. I hold you and I will never let you go. There is value in the coverage of my hands. They span the oceans and I am precise and deliberate in every gesture they extend on your behalf.

My royalty is displayed for you daily. Even though I am The King, my attention is always held by you. You move me to respond. I am attentive to your feelings and your cares.

My entire being yearns to reach out to you in your heartbreaks and seasons of hurt. I am moved with compassion when I see you in any circumstance that limits the potential of who I made you to be.

My compassion for you will never allow me to send you away needing to be provided for. When I watch you struggle, it is evident to those around me that I suffer the deepest agitation in my longing to assist you. I do not seek just to help you in your hurt and crisis, but to reveal to you that I am your ultimate source of strength.

Every road that you take will always bring you back to the undeniable destination of the realization that you need me. I long for you to see that I am your everything.

Always for you,
The King

Date _____

_____

_____

_____

_____

_____

_____

_____

_____

_____

_____

_____

_____

_____

_____

_____

_____

_____

Day 64

> *"His legs are as pillars of marble, set upon sockets of fine gold: his countenance is as Lebanon, as excellent as the cedars."*
>
> **~Song of Solomon 5:15~**
>
> The shepherd girl describes Solomon's legs as strong and powerful and compares his countenance to the cedars of Lebanon. God is perfectly able to carry you over any obstacle on your path ahead. The cross was made from the cedars of Lebanon, and this tells you that God's emotions for you were determined by what was done for you on the cross. It is the cross which directs His actions towards you.

My Love,

I am your strength, and I am fully able to carry you through any circumstance where your feet may fail you.

My feet are firmly planted in the position of opinion that I hold for you. I will never waver in the choice I made to love you with everything I have within me.

My throne is higher than any other throne has ever been or ever will be. There is no power above me and there is nothing that happens without my knowledge or permission. My throne is lifted up and is higher than the hills or the mountains, and everything you see around you is beneath my feet.

Today I ask you to look to me for your strength. Lift up your eyes to the one who resides above the hills for your source of strength.

Look to me in the decision for your paths direction, for I look not just to your present needs but I have already prepared your defense and provision for the circumstances that lie in your path ahead. I have seen what you will need and have already begun providing

Trust in me today. Trust me with your next steps. Trust in my ability to see beyond your level of understanding and rest securely in that trust. I walk before you on your path and my footsteps will never falter. Do not trust your eyes to see your own path's end. Look rather to me and stay your focus on me. I will guide you as I go before you.

Ever before you,
The King

Date _____

_____

_____

_____

_____

_____

_____

_____

_____

_____

_____

_____

_____

_____

_____

_____

_____

_____

_____

Day 65

"His mouth is most sweet: yea, he is altogether lovely. This is my beloved, and this is my friend, o daughters of Jerusalem"
~Song of Solomon 5:16

The shepherd girl closes her description of her groom with the statement, "He is altogether lovely." Describe the features of God to someone today and as you do, describe Him to them like the shepherd girl describes her king. What do you know of God? What can you say of His eyes, hands, arms, and features? What has He shown you of Himself in your life?

My Love,

I love the way you describe me to other people.

Your desire is to help people understand my heart. I love that. There are so many sounds my ears take in every moment, but the sound of you describing me to someone else truly captivates my heart.

You have an impact because those that know who I am to you want to know what it is about me that separate me from all others.

They want to know how you can remain calm in the middle of a crisis and how you are able to stand without fear for what is right. They want to know how you can provide so much strength to others and yet go through a circumstance that causes you to become weak.

They want to know what it is about me that can cause you to smile when you are lonely and to provide for others in your times of loss. They see me when they see you, and although it may cause some to avoid you and some to draw close; it causes all of them to wonder what it is that you have in me.

Today, I want you to tell them of the love that I have for you, and tell them how you see that love demonstrated. Brag on me. So many people are empty and they simply want a relationship that is real. They cover it up in so many ways, but every time they are around you they are all asking in the only ways that they know how to ask, what makes what we have so special. Tell them today!

Forever yours,
The King

Date _____

_____

_____

_____

_____

_____

_____

_____

_____

_____

_____

_____

_____

_____

_____

_____

_____

_____

_____

_____

_____

_____

Day 66

"Whither is thy beloved gone, O thou fairest among women? Whither is thy beloved turned aside? That we may seek him with thee."

~Song of Solomon 6:1~

After the bride describes her groom to those around her, there is an overwhelming offer to help her find him. When others begin to understand who God is to you and they see His impact on your life, they will want to know Him as you do. Do not be afraid to speak of Him to others as He prompts you. The outcome will always produce a hunger in others to know Him.

My Love,

I made you to be seen by others. The more people see of what I have done for you the more they will desire to meet me.

Those around you seek the benefits of what only my relationship can bring, and although they confuse my name with the sources they have chosen; they do not confuse the results that I have given to you as your source.

They understand the results of what I have given to you have produced in your life. They were created to desire me and will never tire in their pursuit for satisfaction until they find me.
They do not know my name, but they know yours. They see what our relationship has brought to you and they recognize the result of that relationship.

I have brought you peace. I have brought you joy, patience, and completion.

You have been made whole and it was my love that completed you.

They have so many substitutes and artificial forms of love that make the authenticity of the love I have given to you stand out so clearly.

When you display that love, you in turn will display me and I will draw all men to me.

Today I ask you to boldly display the fruit of our relationship. It is your name they will ask for and do not mistake their call of your name for the search to find my name.

Show them my name today, my love. Show them how to find me.

Eternally yours,
The King

Date _____

_____
_____
_____
_____
_____
_____
_____
_____
_____
_____
_____
_____
_____
_____
_____
_____
_____
_____

Day 67

> *"My beloved is gone down into his garden, to the beds of spices, to feed in the gardens, and to gather lilies. I am my beloveds' and my beloved is mine: he feedeth among the lilies."*
>
> ~Song of Solomon 6:2-3~
>
> The bride has now taken on Solomon's description of her as her identity. He compares her many times with the flowers and she refers to herself in this passage as such. She sees herself as having been planted and cared for personally by the king with nothing expected of her but to bloom in his care and to accept his love for her. Symbolically, you have been planted by The King where you are at this moment and He planted you so you may be seen and reflect Him to those around you.

My Love,

You are my flower in my garden. You stand out from everyone around you. You are like the lily. You have the potential to grow to tremendous heights, but you are weak in the stem. It is I who gives you strength because you are weak in yourself without me. I took you from among the thorns and planted you in me. It is in my garden that you now flourish and it is here that you are able to see what I have added to you.

I delight in you and I visit you. Today I want you to notice the ways I care for you and open your eyes to the things I have used to strengthen you. Do not fear anything for I am with you.

You are my tender plant that I give my care and attention to; There is nothing that can uproot you from where you are planted. You are mine to care and provide for. When you cannot seem to see me, never doubt that I can see you. I gathered you to plant, sustain, and nurture you; and that is what I will do. You are mine, and I am yours.

Tenderly,
The King

Day 68

> *"Thou art beautiful, O my love, as Tizrah, comely as Jerusalem, terrible as an army with banners."*
>
> **~Song of Solomon 6:4~**
>
> Tizrah belonged to a neighboring province and each year there would be an inspection of the boundaries between Jerusalem and her neighbors. Upon one such inspection, Solomon was said to have looked out at Tizrah and declare it to be beautiful. The rulers of that province, out of fear for Solomon, presented Tizrah to him as a peace offering. When The King of Kings saw you, He declared you beautiful and with that declaration, any power that held you had no choice but to release you into His ownership.

My Love,

I remember when I saw you for the first time and it was in that moment I knew I would find a way to make you forever mine.

You were lost and held captive by sources that had convinced you your identity was found in the things you did, the things you had, and what people thought of you. You were worn out because no matter how hard you worked to find your identity in those sources you were never able to be satisfied.

I remember hearing your cries of frustration, and in each case I painfully sat off to the side until you understood your need to look to me.
I remember that day and it stands out in my mind as one of the greatest days in both of our lives.

You looked up to me.

That was all that it took. I said you were beautiful to me and every force of opposition that held you captive had no choice but to release you. There is no power that could ever keep you from being mine.

There was no struggle when you came to me. It was not a long and drawn out battle of "should I or shouldn't I?" Our eyes connected and you knew you were made for me. Today I want to remind you to think back to that day and remember from what you have been set free.

It is in remembrance of what has been that you find strength for the times which lie before you.

Always yours,
The King

Date _____

_____

_____

_____

_____

_____

_____

_____

_____

_____

_____

_____

_____

_____

_____

_____

_____

_____

Day 69

> *"Turn away thine eyes from me, for they have overcome me: thy hair is as a flock of goats that appear from Gilead."*
>
> **~Song of Solomon 6:5~**
>
> Solomon mentions his bride's eyes quite frequently and this serves to remind you that God wants you to look to Him for every step in this life. He enjoys seeing our eyes because He sees His reflection in them and He is reminded that we exercised free choice to look to Him over every other option we have.

My Love,

I have a confession to make to you. I am absolutely head over heels in love with your eyes.

Love, your eyes are the single most expressive part about you. Your eyes are windows to your very soul. Please don't hide them when we speak. When you talk to me, I cannot help but look deeply you're your eyes every time that we speak.

I watch them all the time, my love, because I am always interested to see what catches them.

What do you like to look at?
What do you see that causes you to turn away your gaze?
What do you see that makes you sad?

What is it you see that reminds you that you are loved by me?

Look for me today!

I want so much to be seen by you, and I cannot wait to look into your eyes and tell you I love you.

I think the thing I love the most about your eyes is that I can see myself in them and sometimes I look into them just to see that reflection. It is my reflection in your eyes that reminds me you chose to look up to me.

The way you lift your eyes to take into view your source of strength and identity is absolutely overwhelming to me!

Eternally yours,
The King

Date _____

_____

_____

_____

_____

_____

_____

_____

_____

_____

_____

_____

_____

_____

_____

_____

_____

_____

Day 70

> "Thy teeth are like as a flock of sheep which go up from the washing, whereof every one bareth twins, and there is not one barren among them"
>
> **~Song of Solomon 6:6~**
>
> In this passage, Solomon is comparing his bride's teeth to the beauty of sheep after they have been bathed. Bright and glistening. What stands out to me here is that Solomon was never a shepherd. He was raised in a royal palace and would not have had the need to see sheep after they had been washed. His bride however did work with sheep and there is no doubt she would have mentioned to him her pleasure at the sight of clean sheep. He was speaking to her in ways she could understand. God is an expert communicator with us. He speaks to us in ways we understand and will never stop reaching out to us where we are.

My Love,

It is so easy for me to communicate with you because I know everything about you.

I know what matters the most to you and I also know the things you could care less about. You have told me things you don't tell anyone, and I have listened. I will always listen to you.

I have been there when you have shown storms of anger, and I have been there when you have been given blue skies of joy. I have been there through it all and nothing has changed or ever will change the depth of love I have for you. I understand you and it is through your language of understanding that I will speak to you.

Look for me today!

I want to guide my voice around every roadblock because I want you to hear me. I want for you to see my love for you in your life. I want you to always be aware of my desire for relationship with you. This journey is not so much about you becoming anything. It is about you un-becoming everything that isn't really you so you can be who you were meant to be in the first place.

Listen for my voice today. I am using everything you have gone through to speak my pleasure and love for you today. I will use things to speak that only you will recognize; this is the true sign to you that I have listened all along to what matters to your heart.

I love you,
The King

Date _____

_____
_____
_____
_____
_____
_____
_____
_____
_____
_____
_____
_____
_____
_____
_____
_____
_____
_____

Day 71

I find it beautiful that Solomon makes mention of her temples again. This is the place on the body where the emotions are easily detected. God is very aware of how you feel and of the things that challenge you emotionally. Your feelings are important to Him and He is protective of your heart. You can trust Him with your feelings and with your emotions.

My Love,

I am all about the details when it comes to you, so is it a wonder that I notice everything about you?

Your heartbeat moves me. I know you as well as I know myself, so is it a wonder that I am moved by the way your heart breaks and moves for those around you? You were designed to express me and give your heart to others in the same way I have given my heart to you. You give it completely and do so knowing, in most cases, your hearts value will fail to be seen by the ones to whom it has been given.

A perfect heart is not one that has never been torn. A perfect heart is one that has been torn and broken multiple times. It is the tears and hurts that make the heart what it was meant to be. Do not stop reaching out to those around you.
Never pass on an opportunity to reflect my expressions of love to you into the lives of others.

It is beautiful to me to watch as you, in spite of misunderstanding by others, reach out and extend a love that could only come as a by-product of my love for you.

Today I want you to take a brief look back at the times where a misunderstanding allowed you to better grow into my image. The more you notice those moments, the more you come to understanding just how expansive my love is for you.

Your feelings, pains, tears, and hurts are never wasted or without value to me. I see everything you go through and I see the feelings you have behind the tears you shed. I am with you, and I could not be more proud of you than I am at this very moment. You express me beautifully!

You are the one that I love,
The King

Date _____

_____
_____
_____
_____
_____
_____
_____
_____
_____
_____
_____
_____
_____
_____
_____
_____
_____
_____
_____

Day 72

> *"There are threescore queens, and fourscore concubines, and virgins without number. My dove, my undefiled is but one; she is the only one of her mother, she is the choice one of her that bare her. The daughters saw her, and blessed her; yea, the queens and the concubines, and they praised her."*

~Song of Solomon 6:8-9~

No matter how out of place the bride would have found herself in the company of the royal wives, there was one undeniable fact she could hold on to. She was chosen by the king. You may feel unworthy of God's love and attention, but you cannot escape the reality that you have been chosen by The King. He chose you knowing everything about you, everything you have done, and everything you will ever do. You have been chosen by The King!

My Love,

I chose you.

So often you look around at others that seem to have qualities befit to royalty and it causes you to lose sight of the fact I have chosen you. I will teach you anything that you need to know about your new life, and I will patiently do so; for in teaching you about this new life, I will in turn teach you who you are to me.

Rest in the confidence of my choice because it was made with all clarity and understanding on my part. There is nothing you could do that would ever have influenced my decision away from you.

You are beautiful. You are complete. You are enough. You are everything I have always wanted. Today as we experience this time together, let me continue to reaffirm to you how valuable you are to me. After I saw you that first time, nothing could keep me from making you mine. I chose you and I chose to pursue you always. I am your very best friend, and life without me is no life at all.

Today I ask you to rest in my choice and my ability to make this choice. You are mine alone and I am so glad you are here to be chose, knowing everything about you I would still choose you again and again. My heart is fixed on you!

Choosing you,
The King

Date _____

_____

_____

_____

_____

_____

_____

_____

_____

_____

_____

_____

_____

_____

_____

_____

_____

_____

Day 73

> *"Who is she that looketh forth as the morning, fair as the moon, clear as the sun, and terrible as an army with banners?"*
>
> **~Song of Solomon 6:10~**
>
> Solomon describes his queen as being someone who stands out in any environment she may find herself. There is a quality about her that draws people's attention to her. You have this ability as well. Your light comes from His Holy Spirit within you and this light allows you to contrast your environment. You are able to bring Him into anyplace you go.

My Love,

I look forward to seeing you each morning. From the moment I see your eyes open I know that bringing you to me was the right decision.

I am not the only one that looks forward to seeing you. There are people you impact every single day, and this morning was no different than any other in that respect. They wait on you, and I do not think you realize just how many people you affect with the light they see in you.

They call you parent, child, sibling, relative, in-law, spouse, church member, employee, co-worker, employer, and friend. I call you mine.

The truth is that it does not matter what the title they refer to you is as much as whom they see in you. To them you are someone who is more than just another customer or co-worker. You are more than just a face that comes and goes in their world. You shine.

The thing that is so attractive about you and the way you shine is that it is completely obvious what you give is not a faked effort on your part. You are genuine. What you have, because of your relationship with me, radiates from you. Like a sunrise against a morning night sky you give off a dazzling light of hope to those in your world.

You reflect a silent strength that is not your own. After the things that you have been through, I am the only way to explain why you are still standing strong. You reflect me to others in everything you do. Today I want you to be who I made you and that is enough. What you will discover is that, when you are yielded to me, you being yourself and me expressing myself are one and the same. I love you. I always have and I always will.

Your source,
The King

Date _____

_____

_____

_____

_____

_____

_____

_____

_____

_____

_____

_____

_____

_____

_____

_____

_____

_____

Day 74

> *"I went down into the garden of nuts to see the fruits of the valley, and to see whether the vine flourished, and the pomegranates budded."*
>
> **~Song of Solomon 6:11~**
>
> This passage is beautiful in the fact it tells the shepherd girls story of finding the king. She lists out where she was going and what she was looking to find. The picture is your life story as well. You set out, at one time, to find things that satisfied your feelings, and like the shepherd girl, there was no mention of intentionally looking for The King. You were caught up in your search for satisfaction and you found what you never thought you would find. You found Him! Your search led you to Him.

My Love,

I have been so aware of you even when there was a time you never had a thought directed towards me.

I remember the very first time we met. It was just like coming home. You looked at me and you said in the deepest place of your heart, "There you are. I finally found you."

As you started on your search and looked to fill the voids of your life, you did not even know I could be real. I watched you go from person to person, place to place, and thing to thing in search of fulfillment. It was a vain search because only I could provide your desires. You went out looking for something completely different, and you did that because you were unaware of me.

Do not let previous searches and their results distract you from what you have finally found with me. Regardless of what you thought you were looking for, you now stand with me and your standing with me will never change.

You are complete in me, and the joy of that completeness that you now enjoy far outweighs the temporary pleasure you were on course to settle for in the sources that were not me.

Your desire is what drove you to find me and it is the desire to be satisfied that took you past so many other substitutes and brought you here with me now. You are mine. We are together and nothing can change that.

All of me,
The King

Date _____

_____

_____

_____

_____

_____

_____

_____

_____

_____

_____

_____

_____

_____

_____

_____

_____

_____

Day 75

> *"Or ever I was aware, my soul made me like the chariots of Amminadib. Return, return, O Shulamite; return, return, that we may look upon thee. What will ye see in the Shulamite? As it were a company of two horses."*
>
> **~Song of Solomon 6:12-13~**
>
> The shepherd girl's desire for satisfaction led her to Solomon's chariot. It was your search for fulfillment that has led you to Him. You have finally found the one whom your soul loves and you knew your search was over when you found Him. Never lose sight of the value of your search. It was necessary in order to bring you to Him.

My Love,

I made you to be seen. Our relationship was made to be seen by everyone around you.

When I came into your life everything about you became new. I radiate from your eyes and your entire disposition became different. The people that know you best see this about you.

The question they are asking is, "Why?" People want to know what took place in your world to make everything so different.

Remember when you were searching for me? Remember how far and wide that search was? You had so many questions and there were so many times that you did not even know how to put into words exactly what you wanted to know. You just knew something was missing. You did not fully understand what it was you were looking for, but you knew in your heart you would know me when you found me.

You desired to find me for who I truly am, and you were relentless in your search.

Your desire to find me has led you to me, and finally you have found everything you were lacking. I completed you. We were meant to be together from the very beginning. Today I ask you to simply enjoy knowing that you finally found me and that we will be together forever. I love you.

                              All of my love,
                              The King

Date _____

_____

_____

_____

_____

_____

_____

_____

_____

_____

_____

_____

_____

_____

_____

_____

_____

_____

_____

Day 76

"How beautiful are thy feet with shoes, O prince's daughter! The joints of thy thighs are like jewels, the work of the hands of a cunning workman."

~Song of Solomon 7:1~

In this passage, Solomon is describing his bride physically. She is thought to be dancing in front of him by the way he is describing her body, however the comparisons to God's view of the believer are stunning. He begins with her feet and the description seems farfetched at first. Her feet are not the feet of royalty, but rather the feet of a field worker. You were always made to be royalty. No matter where your feet have taken you in life, you were always meant to stand before The King.

My Love,

There are two things I want you to be aware of today because the course of your entire day depends upon your understanding of these two things. The first is that you have been made royalty and from the beginning this was always your true identity. Your life was always meant to be one of splendor and grace and my purpose was to restore your birthright. You are not what you feel. You are every bit of what I am telling you at this moment. You are royalty and you are my treasure beyond price. Your feet have taken you down some of the hardest paths. I smile when I think about the grounds they covered and places they have taken you; because your paths in life, no matter how confusing or rough, were designed to bring you to this path that you now walk with me. You walk beside me and your heart is mine. Your path was always meant to be one walked in an understanding of who you are to me. When you grasp just how important you are to me, every path you take becomes a trail of light because you now know you have never walked alone.

The second thing you need to know is that, as a part of the body of Christ, I love watching you move. You were designed without flaw and then added to the body for a reason because you were made to move. I made you royalty to enable you to walk in places that desperately need to see royalty. Never be ashamed to move within the body of Christ. Never be embarrassed or allow feelings of inadequacy to prevent you from moving in the ways you were designed to move. Shame for paths that your feet used to walk can prevent you from walking new paths with me. Walk with me today and let me prove your new identity to you.

Your reason,
The King

Date _____

Day 77

> *"Thy navel is like a round goblet, which wanteth not liquor: thy belly is like a heap of wheat set about with lilies."*

> **~Song of Solomon 7:2~**

The word navel is the word "Mixing Basin". To make wine palatable in those days, you would pour hot wine and cold water into such a basin and mix it together. The Wine pictures God's law which was too strong to drink. The Water represents His Spirit which now indwells you. Jesus was the mixing basin who cried out, "If any man thirst, let him come to me." Blood and water mingled together so that we could be satisfied. This terminology was symbolic of physical health. When Solomon's bride would breathe, her shirt would lift above her navel and that stirred him. The very act of you breathing stirs God's heart because you embody spiritual health. What a beautiful picture.

My Love,

When I look at you I see the most beautiful vessel to ever come before my eyes.

Hot wine and fresh water mingled together is the most beautiful way to describe physical health, and when I see you breathe I thrill because I have completely healed you and you wear that healing so beautifully. I have made you clean and no longer will a crippling fallen nature have its way in you. You are no longer a victim of your circumstances, but you are now a victor. I have given you a new heart, a new nature, and you have a new purpose.

When you physically breathe I see spiritual health embodied in front of me, and it stirs my heart like no other.

Today I want you to breathe deeply for me and know I see purity and grace in you. I see health and vitality of spirit where once there was darkness. You are a new creation now and a vessel created unto honor.

I am well pleased with you.

I will never find displeasure in you because you are hidden in Christ. Breathe deeply today. With each breath, remind yourself, after all that you have been through, you are spiritually well. You are my redeemed love.

Your reason,
The King

Date _____

_____

_____

_____

_____

_____

_____

_____

_____

_____

_____

_____

_____

_____

_____

_____

_____

_____

_____

Day 78

> "Thy two breasts are like young roes that are twins."
>
> **~Song of Solomon 7:3~**
>
> Solomon describes his bride's completeness. There was nothing about her that caused him to turn away. The King of Kings declares you are complete in Him. There is nothing you could ever do to turn away His attention from you. You are not what you feel, but rather what His word reveals.

My Love,

I have begun a good work in you and I am faithful to complete that work in you.

Relationship with me has brought you your identity. You are completely planted and based in me. I am who I say I am and I have done what I said I will do. The more you deepen in your understanding of just who you are to me and who I am to you the more you will reflect my very nature.

People will look at you and see my attributes. They will see beauty and grace. They will see a perfect combination of faith and love expressed in you. Your relationship with me has added and will continue to add opportunities for you to minister this strength to those who watch you. They live in your house, they attend your church, they shop at your market, and they notice you. They look at the attributes I have added to your spirit and they see in you the things that our relationship has given to you.

Today I want you to walk confidently in the paths I lay before you and be aware that people are looking to you because they want to know what made you the way you are. Do not be afraid to speak of how our relationship has changed you and added to you. They are coming because they see not you, but me in you and they like what they see.

Know that people see you the way I see you, and if you ever doubt that, just ask me and I will remind you.

Yours completely,
The King

Date _____

_____
_____
_____
_____
_____
_____
_____
_____
_____
_____
_____
_____
_____
_____
_____
_____
_____
_____
_____
_____
_____
_____
_____
_____

Day 79

> *"Thy neck is as a tower of ivory; thine eyes like the fishpools in heshbon, by the gate of Bathrabbim: thy nose is as a tower of Lebanon which looketh toward Damascus."*
>
> **~Song of Solomon 7:4~**
>
> This passage pictures God's description of us so well. He knows our frailties and our weaknesses in our flesh, but He also knows that beneath our weaknesses lies His strength. He is our strength and places us where He does in life to help those around us receive His strength through us.

My Love,

I made you to be a person of beautiful contrasts, and it is in those contrasts that I am fully able to be expressed.

You are a tower of strength that I have placed directly where weakness is prevalent. Sometimes you question the places I have set you and the peoples I have chosen to place you among. I place you in the midst of weakness so you can show others the strength I provide. They see you and they have a chance to see I valued them enough to plant my love directly in their path. They may not recognize my hand in their life by your presence, but there will be a day when they do.

You are strong. Ivory is beautiful to look at, and yet it is fragile. There will be times when you feel broken, but that is merely a surface emotion. I provide you with internal strength and you will never be destroyed. Stand where you have been placed and direct others to your source of strength.

When I look in your eyes, I see this understanding reflected. In a desert, nothing stirs a heart more than a glimmer of water. This is sought after and your eyes reflect a refreshing compassion that comes from a deep source within. You will always attract others with this refreshment.

Today I ask that you remember the source of your strength and compassion. You have been fully equipped to express me to those that cross your path. Do not hesitate to give to others what I have given to you.

Yours in everything,
The King

Date _____

_____

Day 80

> "Thine head upon thee is like Caramel, and the hair of thine head like purple; the king is held in the galleries."
>
> ~Song of Solomon 7:5~
>
> I love the way Solomon words his admiration of his bride. He tells her that she holds him captive and he cannot look away from her when he is near her. Caramel was a mountain that would always draw the eyes in admiration of those who passed by. You hold God's attention. He is drawn to you and created you to be seen by others. You reflect His majesty and power. He is held by you.

My Love,

When people look at other people, even with the best of intentions, they tend to make a judgment about them.

Judgment of their value is awarded based upon a myriad of different criteria. Do they look worthy of love? Do they behave worthy of my attention? Do they fully appreciate effort extended on their behalf?

The problem with this judgment is that it is not from me. I looked at you with the intention and action of loving you, knowing you would not always look to me, and fully aware it would not be a fair exchange of return. I did not love you because of what you could do to justly merit my love. I loved you because I wanted to make you worthy. You are worthy.

I made you majestic and others will look to you for inspiration. Today I want you to be aware of where I have placed you. I have placed my inspiration within your heart and that in turn has been on display for others to benefit. They will look up to you and this is your opportunity to direct them to look up past you to see the very source of your strength. I have made you inspiring now and you are perfectly adorned in the glory and the elegance that I provide for you.

My spirit dwells within you and I will never leave you. I am held by my love for you. Look at others with awareness of the value I have for them and help them understand what I feel for them.

Yours in everything,
The King

Date _____

Day 81

> *"How fair and how pleasant art thou, O love, for delights! This thy stature is like to a palm tree, and thy breasts to clusters of grapes. I said, I will go up to the palm tree, I will take hold of the boughs thereof: now also thy breasts shall be as clusters of the vine and the smell of thy nose like apples;"*
>
> **~Song of Solomon 7:6-8~**
>
> Solomon is expressing his satisfaction in his bride and I find a beautiful picture of the heart of God for you. He is satisfied with you and He genuinely enjoys you and being around you.

My Love,

Your gracefulness and sweetness is admired and sought after by those that find themselves in your company. When I describe you, the most pleasant things come to mind. I brought you into this relationship with me because I genuinely enjoy you. I thrill at you and you satisfy me. There is not one thing you can do to intrigue me more than to be who I made you to be. The greatest thing you will ever learn to understand is how complete and overwhelming my love for you is. It is relentless in its pursuit of you and nothing can find a way around its protective walls to get to you.

My love for you is kind, patient, steadfast, and true. It is the greatest delight of your heart, and it is my greatest accomplishment in giving it to you. I love you. My relationship with you provided you with, not only a new future, but a new past as well. Your past starts at the cross. There is nothing that holds you back from enjoying all that I am.

Today, I ask that you take joy in what we have together. Never allow anyone to convince you I feel anything less than the greatest love for you. Today I ask you to allow me to show you just how steadfastly that my eyes are fixed on you.

I love you,
The King

Day 82

> *"And the roof of thy mouth like the best wine for my beloved, that goeth down sweetly, causing the lips of those that are asleep to speak."*

> **~Song of Solomon 7:9~**

> Solomon enjoyed sharing conversation with his bride because she created within him the desire to communicate to her his thoughts as well as hear her thoughts. God loves to hear you speak and it evokes within Him the desire to communicate His love back to you. You have a way of speaking God's truths in a way that opens doors in the hearts of those who listen to you. This is your God given gift and when you exercise that gift, you are helping others to hear God's voice.

My Love,

I love the way you think and process your thoughts because it is individually unique, and when paired with your personality it becomes powerful.

This relationship has given you so many things of value which you have yet to discover. One of those things is the understanding of just how valuable your personality is to me. You speak unlike anyone else because your words originate from your heart in a way unique to you. You process and present your thoughts so individually and it is powerful!

I watch you as people discuss me, and I can see in your eyes a longing to have the confidence to express to others just how much of me you enjoy and what I have taught you about me. You stay quiet so many times because you feel intimidated, but your thoughts are worth far more than you give credit. I placed those views of understanding in your heart for the reason of expressing them outwardly.

175

There are people asleep all around you. They are oblivious to how much they mean to me. Your voice, expressing all I have taught you about me, is what is needed to cause them to wake up.

Wake them up today!

Speak to them of what you have learned and are learning of my nature and desire for a relationship with you. What have I taught your heart about me? What have I shown you of my kingdom? Speak it today because people that are asleep have no idea how much they are missing while they are asleep!

Ever for you,
The King

Date _____

_____
_____
_____
_____
_____
_____
_____
_____
_____
_____
_____
_____
_____
_____
_____
_____

Day 83

> *"I am my beloveds, and his desire is toward me. Come, my beloved, let us go forth into the field; let us lodge in the villages. Let us get up early to the vineyards; let us see if the vine flourish, whether the tender grape appear, and pomegranates bud forth: there will I give thee my loves. The mandrakes give a smell, and at our gates are all manner of pleasant fruits, new and old, which I have laid up for thee, O my beloved"*
>
> **~Song of Solomon 7:10-13**
>
> The bride is speaking to Solomon and expressing her desire to bring him into the places of her past that impacted her the most. When you grasp the depth of God's love for you, you want to take The King of Kings into every area of your life and you desire for Him to share in every experience that you have. He is truly your life.

My Love,

You are absolutely mine and I am without a doubt yours. The more you learn what this statement truly means, the more that you will begin to see that you are never without me and nothing could ever come between us. I want to experience everything that you experience and I want to see all of the sights you see. I am here because I want us to be together.

Make the early times of the day "our time". Before the struggles and distractions of the day begin, when all is still, just take a few moments to meditate on the fact that you are mine and that I am yours. Take this knowledge with you as we see the potential to come in the day ahead of us. Let me show you all I have been waiting to show you today.

I have everything under control, and no matter what you see as you start the day with me; please know I am right beside you and there is nothing you will ever face alone. Look for me today and know that my desire is towards you!

Yours in everything,
The King

Day 84

> *"His left hand should be under my head, and his right hand should embrace me."*
>
> **~Song of Solomon 8:3~**
>
> The bride verbalizes Solomon's ability to satisfy her. He knows exactly how she receives love. The picture is beautiful because it is the perfect combination of security and intimacy. God provides this for you. in holding you close in protection while seeking to satisfy your every need.

My Love,

I look into your heart and I see what you truly wish to find in this relationship, and I am fully capable of making what you desire from me a constant reality.

I am able to do what no one else can do. I look into your heart, my love, and I see you long for me and an understanding of my presence. You long to know that you are safe, valued, and loved.

When you started on this journey of discovery there was no end to your thirst, and I watched as you approached each well with a hope in your heart that you could be satisfied in your search. I watched you discover each well was empty, and at every turn I reached out to you. Every moment you were in my sight, and as you would reach point after point of discouragement I spoke to your heart.

You heard me each and every time although you did not always know it was me speaking. I speak to you now as I tell you this; you are mine and I will never let you go. I offer you security and I find value in you.

I am able to satisfy the cry of your heart for these things you seek and will never stop revealing them to you. Rest in me today and rest in the understanding that you have finally found me. You are in my arms and nothing can ever take you from this place of refuge. I alone brought you to me. Just as there was nothing you could ever do to earn what I have given you, there is nothing that you can do to make you unworthy of what you now possess. You are royalty. You are loved.

All of me,
The King

Date _____

_____
_____
_____
_____
_____
_____
_____
_____
_____
_____
_____
_____
_____
_____
_____
_____
_____
_____
_____

Day 85

> *"I charge you, o daughters of Jerusalem that ye stir not up, nor awake my love, until he please."*
>
> ~Song of Solomon 8:4~
>
> To live for God is to live your life in the constant effort to try to please him through acts of service and striving to gain His affirmation. To live from God is to realize that you already possess His approval and His complete affirmation. You rest in the fact that He made you acceptable in His sight and you find rest in Him.

My Love,

The greatest gift I give you in this relationship we share is rest.

The search for significance, security, and intimacy is over. You have worked so hard to try to earn these things from me, and the most difficult thing you have to overcome is the understanding that I require nothing from you.

I do not need you to live for me one more moment of your life. In fact, I have never wanted you to live for me. It sounds so good to live for me, but I do not need that from you nor do I want it. I have hands that are more than capable of work, and they are much more careful than even the best intentioned. My feet can go places yours cannot. I ask you to stop working so hard to live for me and that you instead that you determine to live from me.

Living from me and living for me are two different things. To live for me is to try to earn my approval while living from me is to operate in the knowledge that you already have my approval. You already please me. The more you seek to know me the more you will understand the difference between knowing me and understanding me.

To know me is to know my heart for you. You came to me with nothing, and before you came to me I had already decided how I felt about you. I made you holy and I made you right with me. There was nothing you could do to ever accomplish such a feat, and there is nothing you could do to undo what I made you.

Rest in me today and rest in who I made you. Rest in the understanding that nothing can ever make you less than what I made you.

Always here for you,
The King

Date _____

_____
_____
_____
_____
_____
_____
_____
_____
_____
_____
_____
_____
_____
_____
_____
_____
_____
_____
_____
_____
_____

Day 86

My Love,

Never be ashamed of the time you spent in the wilderness. I am not intimidated by your seasons of wilderness wandering. There is a tendency for people to miss out on just how valuable the wilderness experience is in developing the relationship you have with me.

You went into the wilderness alone and came out of the wilderness with me. You went into the wilderness with your identity based upon what you did and emerged with your identity based on who I made you. You went into the wilderness simply who you were, but came out of the wilderness exactly who I made you to be. It is in the wilderness my voice can stand out in contrast, and the wilderness can shape you in ways that the palace never could.

The wilderness can be a place where you are forced to understand just how filling and satisfying I am; because the wilderness reveals for what you are truly thirsting. It is a place where identity is discovered and trust is solidified. The result of the wilderness is the understanding of your total dependence on me.

One of the single greatest outcomes of your wilderness experience is that it was there we met. You emerged with your identity in me established and those who know you best can see the person they now interact with is no longer the same.

You are royalty now. You are able to understand my fingerprint has been on your entire life, and you can see all the ways I have been reaching out to you. I used your wilderness to help you understand you never have to go to the wilderness again. You found me! Enjoy the relationship your wilderness brought to you.

All of me,
The King

Date _____

_____
_____
_____
_____
_____
_____
_____
_____
_____
_____
_____
_____
_____
_____
_____
_____
_____
_____
_____

Day 87

> *"Set me as a seal upon thine heart, as a seal upon thine arm: for love is strong as death; jealously is cruel as the grave: the coals thereof are coals of fire, which hath a most vehement flame."*

~Song of Solomon 8:6~

You can survive anything if you have a firm understanding of how much God loves you. The seal she is speaking of was a bracelet that would be worn on the upper portion of the left arm. The left arm was closest to the heart and the bracelet symbolized that the hand was directed by what was known in the heart. You will present the God that you know and it is vital that you seal your understanding of His ever present love for you deep into your heart. Your actions will stem from this understanding.

My Love,

I want you to lock something into your heart and mind and never let it slip away from your understanding. I love you.

I know everything there is to know about you and I love you. I made the choice about how I felt about you a long time ago, and there is nothing you can do or not do to change the fact that I love you.

Today I want you to forgive yourself for the mistakes you have made in the past and to let those moments go. I made you clean and new when I brought you to me, and you are defined now by who I am and not by who you are or what you have done. My love, I ask that you seal this knowledge in your heart and determine you will never let it go for anything or anyone.

You wear my love for you and you wear my grace. My strength and honor will be your clothing, and wherever you go, you are carrying me with you. I will forever define you. No matter the changing opinions those around you may hold of you, you are mine and you always shall be.

I am jealous for you and your attention. I am protective of you and you wear my seal upon you. No one can ever remove hope to erase what I have made permanent. No action can ever reverse my decision to love you, and nothing can keep me from being with you.

Never forget how much I adore you. You are mine, and I am completely yours.

Eternally,
The King

Date _____

_____
_____
_____
_____
_____
_____
_____
_____
_____
_____
_____
_____
_____
_____
_____
_____
_____

Day 88

> *"Many waters cannot quench love; neither can the floods drown it: if a man would give all the substance of his house for love, it would be utterly contemned."*
>
> **~Song of Solomon 8:7~**
>
> This passage is being spoken by the richest man in the world. He was in full recognition of the beauty and value of true love in a relationship. You have true love in its entirety in your relationship with The King of Kings. This is His gift to you and you will always hold it in your possession. It was given by the one who truly knows its value even on the days when you fail to see it.

My Love,

I have one consuming objective in this relationship I share with you. It fills my every thought and action. I desire to show you just how much I love you.

I will stop at nothing in my pursuit to capture your heart and teach you just how deep and vast my love for you is. I am relentless in my search to demonstrate this great affection for you.

My love for you is a fire that can never be extinguished. Its radiant glow is warm and its light can penetrate the darkest place you could ever find yourself. There is no such thing as a substitution when it comes to my love for you. My love is a flame that lives to burn for you. It will always draw you to it for you were made to possess it.

There is not a depth you can go where my love could not find you. There is nothing that you could find to cover you from my love's redemptive, cleansing power. You will always be able to see my fingerprint in your life. No matter where you go or what you do, that fingerprint will always speak of my love for you.

You cannot buy my love nor could you find a greater love in any other source.

When you found me, you truly found everything you'll ever need. I gave you my love and will not rest in my efforts to communicate to you just how expansive and vast my love for you is.

In pursuit of you,
The King

Date _____

_____

Day 89

> *"We have a sister, and she hath no breasts: what shall we do for our sister in the day when she shall be spoken for? If she be a wall, we will build upon her a palace of silver: if she be a door, we will enclose her with boards of cedar."*
>
> ~Song of Solomon 8: 8-9~
>
> The question is asked to Solomon, "What if your bride does not feel complete or of value?" This question can be applied to you, and I as we view the relationship with The King. The answer is powerful! The walls represent the areas of strength and the doors represent those areas of our lives where we find a weakness. The cedar represents the cross. God will always build upon our areas of strength and cover our weaknesses in the power of His cross.

My Love,

There will always be times when you feel as though you do not measure up or somehow lack what you need to merit value to me. It is in those times I want you to remember what I am about to tell you.

You have looked at who you are and you have found yourself to be incomplete and this is where I come in.

I know everything about you and I see your strengths. It is upon those strengths I will build you and provide increase. In those areas of your life you will exhibit me the best.

I will encompass and hide the weakness and the vulnerabilities you possess, within the protection my cross has provided. The areas where you feel the most vulnerable and weak are the areas I will surround and strengthen with the knowledge of who I am. Your weaknesses become the platform for my strength.

There is nothing that I cannot protect you from.

Completing you,
The King

Day 90

> *"Thou that dwellest in the gardens, the companions hearken to thy voice: cause me to hear it."*
>
> ~Song of Solomon 8:13~
>
> This last passage gives a request that The King longs to hear. It is the request to help us understand His voice when He speaks. God is speaking in beyond audible ways each and every day. Ask Him to help you hear His voice every moment of the day and you will be amazed at how plainly He has been speaking to your heart your whole life.

My Love,

I love to hear you speak, and when you say my name my heart melts.

I created beauty. I made it grow and flourish where no one else could; and there in the middle of what I created I placed you. You blend in with every bit of beauty I created, and yet you stand out because your beauty is like none other. The sound of your voice and the way you pronounce your words is beautiful to listen to.

The day begins and everything seems still and calm, and then you speak. You speak, and there is nothing in this world that could prevent me from listening. I love when you tell me what you have on your heart and mind. When you speak to me about the things closest to you it is one of the most powerful demonstrations of faith you could give. You speak them to me because you trust me with your fears, worries, heartbreaks, and feelings. It is an amazing faith on your part to speak to me about these things because it shows me you have chosen me over every other option in your life.

There is nothing you could tell me to change the way that I feel about you. Please know I want you to talk to me about anything and everything. I love when you get passionate about the things that stir you most because it is then your heart is the most open.

Talk to me today. Talk to me about everything, and know the words your heart speaks are being taken in by mine.

I want nothing more than to be your everything. I am focused on you. I always have been, my love, and I always will be. I cannot wait to hear from you today.

Your one true love,
The King

Date _____

_____
_____
_____
_____
_____
_____
_____
_____
_____
_____
_____
_____
_____
_____
_____
_____
_____
_____